William Holmes McGuffey, John Menaul

Laguna Indian Translation of McGufeyf's New First Eclectic Reader

William Holmes McGuffey, John Menaul

Laguna Indian Translation of McGufeyf's New First Eclectic Reader

ISBN/EAN: 9783337016265

Printed in Europe, USA, Canada, Australia, Japan

Cover: Foto ©Paul-Georg Meister /pixelio.de

More available books at **www.hansebooks.com**

LAGUNA INDIAN TRANSLATION

of

MC GUFFEY'S NEW FIRST ECLECTIC READER.

TRANSLATED AND PRINTED

BY

JOHN MENAUL.

LAGUNA, ~~NEW~~ MEXICO.

1882.

INTRODUCTION

The object in translating and printing this little School Book is to enable the Laguna Indian children who attend school, to understand the English which they are learning in the Government Day School. "Mc Guffey's New First Eclectic Reader" has been selected for translation, because it was pretty well adapted to the work, and because it was being taught in the School as a Text Book.

The work would be much more satisfactory if the words were separated into syllables by hyphens; but as it is very desirable that the contents of each page of the English should be represented on the opposite page of the translation, we could not uniformly, so separate them into syllables for want of space.

In adopting a mode of spelling for the Laguna Language, our endeavor has been to use only the letters necessary to represent the Indian sounds as given by the Interpreter, (see the Alphabet for the sounds of the letters). But in this, as in all unwritten languages, many difficulties present themselves as soon as an attempt is made to reduce the language to writing. The same word is often given under several modifications when, to an English mind, it ought to mean just the same thing and be written in the same way. These modifications are caused by the different connections in which the word is used as related to other words in the same sentence, or to different ideas in different sentences, by singular, dual or plural nominative and objective cases, by affirmative or negative assertions, or in asking a question.

Again when modifications are expected and apparently necessary, there may not be any, the peculiar idiom and formation of the Language not requiring changes where we would expect them.

It is often a question whether a word should end in *a* or *ah*, in *e* or *eh*, *ĕ* or *ĕh*; or whether they should be written at all when they have only a breathed sound. In all such cases we have written the words or syllables so that we could read them ourselves wherever or in whatever connection we found them. When we could not thus read them, the spelling has been changed for one more in conformity with the true sound. We had to follow this course for want of linguistic authority on the subject.

Again, there are many click sounds which cannot be represented by our letters. These will, in time, drop out of the Language, but their place must now be supplied by sounds which can be written, and at the same time, be intelligible to the native ear.

The greatest difficulty, in this connection, consists in the unsettled state of the Language itself, especially in the vowel sounds. This is owing to the total want of records or writing of any kind among the people; thus necessitating the Translator to depend upon the Interpreter who, in this case, being unable to read or write, can not give an analysis of even the commonest word.

The greatest difficulty in getting a literal translation consists in the want of prepositions, conjunctions etc. in the Laguna Language, and the want of equivalents of very many of our common ideas and words. The Language is very full as far as the daily customs and avocations of *these* people are concerned but exceedingly meager outside of that sphere.

The work of translating this book has been done through the Spanish Language, and has been rendered as literal as the Laguna idiom etc. would permit. The greater part of the translating was done some two years ago, and has since been used in the Day School in connection with the English as a means of enabling the scholars to understand what they read. The work of printing has extended over a year. I have done the type setting and press work in the intervals of Day School hours as opportunity permitted.

On this account, there is neither that degree of accuracy nor uniformity in spelling that is to be desired in such a work. As we advanced in the work the pronunciation of many words became plainer to us, and thus necessitated a change in spelling. We were also, becoming better able to detect those sounds only lightly articulated by the Interpreter, and the Interpreter himself was becoming better acquainted with the work of translating; yet the work as, a whole, is as near correct as we could expect under the attending circumstances.

John Menaul.
Laguna,
Valencia Co.
Feb. 20th 1882.   New Mexico.

ECLECTIC EDUCATIONAL SERIES.

McGUFFEY'S NEW
FIRST ECLECTIC READER:
FOR YOUNG LEARNERS.

By WM. H. McGUFFEY, LL. D.

VAN ANTWERP, BRAGG & CO.,

137 WALNUT STREET,　　　28 BOND STREET,
CINCINNATI　　　　　　　NEW YORK.

Entered according to Act of Congress, in the year 1857, by W. B. SMITH, in the Clerk's Office of the District Court of the United States, for the Southern District of Ohio.

Entered according to Act of Congress, in the year 1863, by
SARGENT, WILSON & HINKLE,
In the Clerk's Office of the District Court of the United States, for the Southern District of Ohio.

ECLECTIC PRESS:
VAN ANTWERP, BRAGG & CO.,
CINCINNATI.

LAGUNA INDIAN TRANSLATION OF MC GUFFEY'S NEW FIRST ECLECTIC READER.

THE ALPHABET.

A a   as a in far   AI ai as ai in aid
CH ch as ch in church   CK ck as ck in cackle
D d   as d in dread   E   e   as e in then
E ē   as ee in see   E   ĕ   as e in echo
EA ea as ea in teach   EI ei as ei in eider
H h   as h in hoot   I   i   as i in pick
K k   as k in kick   L   l   as l in lull
M m   as m in mum   N   n   as n in nun
Ñ ñ   nasal   ÑY ñy as Spanish ñ
O o   as o in note   P   p   as p in pipe
R r   as r in roaring   S   s   as s in sauce
SH sh as sh in should   SK sk as sk in skate
T t   as t in tramp   TH th as th in thank
ʇ   as tdh or t in Spa. tu ty as kty, as one sound
U u   as u in but   W   w   as w in wish
Y y   as y in year   Z   z   as z in zone.

THE ALPHABET.

a	A	*a*	n	N	*n*
b	B	*b*	o	O	*o*
c	C	*c*	p	P	*p*
d	D	*d*	q	Q	*q*
e	E	*e*	r	R	*r*
f	F	*f*	s	S	*s*
g	G	*g*	t	T	*t*
h	H	*h*	u	U	*u*
i	I	*i*	v	V	*v*
j	J	*j*	w	W	*w*
k	K	*k*	x	X	*x*
l	L	*l*	y	Y	*y*
m	M	*m*	z	Z	*z*

A a		AX ax	F f	FAN fan
B b		BOX box	G g	GIRL girl
C c		CAT cat	H h	HEN hen
D d		DOG dog	I i	INK ink
E e		ELK elk	J j	JUG jug

LAGUNA INDIAN TRANSLATION OF MC GUFFEY'S NEW FIRST ECLECTIC READER.　　Page 8

A a AX ax | F f FAN fan
Opkowañye | Opopots

B b BOX box | G g GIRL girl
Kasha | Makutsa

C c CAT cat | H h HEN hen
Musa | Kwako

D d DOG dog | I i INK ink
Tēya | Omistchits

E e ELK elk | J j JUG jug
Tyusha | Ṣpuna

Page 9 — LAGUNA INDIAN TRANSLATION OF MC GUFFEY'S NEW FIRST ECLECTIC READER.

K k KID kid
Karawash

P p PIG pig
Kochēno

L l LARK lark
Lark

Q q QUAIL quail
Kwas*t*oēts

M m MAN man
Hutstse

R r RAT rat
Suña

N n NUT nut
Tyeiañye

S s SUN sun
Oshatcha

O o OX ox
Weyes

T t TUB tub
Asa

K k	KID kid	P p	PIG pig
L l	LARK lark	Q q	QUAIL quail
M m	MAN man	R r	RAT rat
N n	NUT nut	S s	SUN sun
O o	OX ox	T t	TUB tub

| U | URN | X | EX |
| u | urn | x | ex |

| V | VINE | Y | YOKE |
| v | vine | y | yoke |

| W | WREN | Z | ZEBRA |
| w | wren | z | zebra |

MODEL PRONOUNCING EXERCISE,

Embracing all the words found in Lesson I, on the following page.

I	in	do	we	he
it	on	go	am	my
is	an	no	ox	up

LAGUNA INDIAN TRANSLATION OF MC GUFFEY'S NEW FIRST ECLECTIC READER.

U u URN urn
Weistañye

X x EX ex
Ex

V v VINE vine
Tsēkeiyow

Y y YOKE yoke
Ayow*t*yuisht

W WREN wren
Sut*t*ye

Z ZEBRA zebra
Zebra

Hinome keia epech hinometitch he it *t*yu thoko imme sashe imme iske sah weyes tinyeae

LESSON I.

Immĕṭa ṭua iske weyes?
ṭua immetsa iske weyes.
ṭua imme satyashe weyes..

Nutyĕĕko ṭochosa hinometitch?
How ṭyu nutyĕĕko ṭochosa hinometitch?
Hinometitch how ṭyu nutyĕĕya ṭochosa.

Eikeia ṭyĕĕcho hinome?
Tĕ keia ṭyĕĕcho hinome?
Hinome imme eikeia ṭyĕĕcho.

LESSON I.

Let the child spell each word in the line, then read the line.

SPELL.	READ.
is it an ox	Is it an ox?
it is an ox	It is an ox.
it is my ox	It is my ox.
do we go	Do we go?
do we go up	Do we go up?
we do go up	We do go up.
am I in	Am I in?
am I in it	Am I in it?
I am in it	I am in it.

LESSON II.*

Is it an ax?
It is an ax.
It is my ax.
Is it by me?
My ax is by me. So it is.

Is he in?	It is I.
He is in.	It is he.
Is he by me?	We do it.
Do we go in?	Do as we do.

* Spell each word in the line; then read the line, as in Lesson I.

LESSON II.

Immeṭa ṭua iske opkowañye?
ṭua immetsa iske opkowañye.
ṭua immetsa sopkowanye.
Howĕko sṭya sēpsho hinome opkowañye?
Sopkowañye imme howĕko sēpsho hinome.
Ha imme tēska.

Eikeia ṭyacho?	Imme ṭo hinome.
Eikeia ka.	Wa immetsa.
Immeṭa howĕko sṭya sēpsho hinome?	Hinometitch enyechana.
Nutyĕpo ṭochosa hinometitch keia?	Epech immeĕ hinometitch esetchanatshe

1

LESSON III.

Iske kowe̱oñyeme kaiechonye kwako.
Itye kwako nĕyo̱tyo?

Iske tsanawañye tĕya.
Tĕya kakoh iske hutstse.

Iske sitchu weyes.
Cha̱owe sopĕ.

Iske kisha̱a kochēno
Itye kochēno ñomēts̱tyo?

Iske kukañye waksh.
Eicheish waksh ashañye sewas̱tyañye.

LESSON III.*

A sly hen.
Can she fly?

A bad dog.
It bit a man.

A big ox.
Let him go.

A fat pig.
Can it run?

A red cow.
Has she hay?

---

* Spell each word in the line; then read, as in Lesson I.

LESSON IV.*

 Can the cat get the rat?

 See the rat. Was it hid?

 See the kid. Can it run?

 A sly fox. He had a hen.

 An old ape. Can he hop?

* Spell each word in the line; then read, as in Lesson I.

LESSON IV.

Itye musa nityaṭyo suña?

Sēokutch suña.
Choēskomush suña?

Sēokutch karawash washṭye.
Itye karawash washṭyē nyomētsṭyo?

Iske koweṭoñyeme kaiechoñye masṭya.
Masṭya keikakah iṣke kwako.

Iske hustchētsa ape.
Itye noṭotsṭaṭyu ape?

LESSON V.

Immeṭa ṭua iske eistchustche? ṭua immetsa iske eistchustche. Immeṭa ṭua seistchustche? ṭua imme seistchustche. Musa washṭye imme howka seistchustche.

Iske opopots ka Ann. Itye hishome ñyopopotsañyeṭyoma hinome? Hinome itye ñypopotsañyeshoma hishome. Hishome itye ñyopopotsañyeshoma hinome. Hishome ṭyopopotsañe hinome.

LESSON VI.

Hinome sēokutch iske kavayo. Itye hishome ñyokutchsho kavayo? Ha, ha, hinome ñyokutchse. Kavayo itye ñyomētsko. Muh kavayo, O, sēokutch kavayo komētsa!

Hinome sēokutch iske kochēno. Kwae imme skeie kishaṭa kochēno! Itye kochēno ñyomētstyo? Kochēno satse itye ñyomētskoño. Kochēno imme skeie kishaṭa satse itye ñyo mētskoño.

LESSON V.

Is it a bed?
It is a bed.
Is it for me?
It is for me.
Kit is on my bed.

A fan for Ann.
Can you fan me?
I can fan you.
You can fan me.
You do fan me.

LESSON VI.

I see a nag.
Do you see it?
Yes, yes, I do.
The nag can run.
See it, O, see it run!

I see a pig.
How fat it is!
Can the pig run?
It can not run.
It is too fat to run.

LESSON VII.

An old log hut.
A new log hut.
Is it for me?
Is it for you?
It is for us.

See my fat ox.
Is it an old ox?
It is an old ox.
It is not a red ox.
It is a dun ox.

A sly old ape.
It has a nut.
Get it for me.
May I get it?
Yes, if you can.

O, see the fly!
How it can fly!
It bit an old ox.
Can the fly run?
Yes! run, fly, run!

LAGUNA INDIAN TRANSLATION OF
MC GUFFEY'S NEW FIRST ECLECTIC READER.

LESSON X.

Iske sawĕñye kowwoh koats.
Iske natse kowwoh koats.
Immeṯa sowwoh hinome?
Immeṯa chuchowwoh hishome?
Imme suchaowwoh.

Sēokutch satyashe weyes kishaṯa.
Immeṯa ṯua iske hustchĕtsa weyes?
Imme iske hustchĕtsa weyes.
ṯua imme weyes satse kukañyesho.
ṯua imme iske kwĕme kukañye weyes.

Iske koweṯoñyeme kaiechoñye hustchĕtsa ape.
Ape kaikoiya iske ṯyeiañye.
Howe keikome ṯyeiañye koyotseme hinome.
Itye hinome neiyowotye nitṯaṯye ṯyeiañye?
Ha, hishome itye kowko.

O, sēokutch tsape!
Kwae itye tsape tseaṯa!
Tsape kako iske hustchĕtsa weyes.
Itye tsape ñyomĕtstyo?
Ha! ñyomĕtsko, tsape, ñyomĕtsko!

LESSON VIII.

Immeṭa ṭua iske waksh?
ṭua immetsa iske waksh.
ṭua imme satyashe waksh.
Waksh satse hate ashañye sewastchañye.
Pityesha waksh ashañye sewastchañye.

Hinome sĕokutch iske asa.
Asa imme tseya.
Itye hishome heya nowyastchĕsho?
Ha, hinome itye.
Hinome itye heya nowyastchĕse.

O, sĕokutch satyashe musa!
Musa imme eitinyeañu stchu ka iske eistchustche.
Musa kokutcha iske suña.
Suña kokutcha musa.
Suña komĕts kotyeiṭye.

Sĕokutch sashe natse keiskuucheiko.
Kwae itye keiskuucheiko katsa.
Hishome itye ñyenaṭacho iske.
Satse nowĕṭaanyekweashoño iske.
Hinome satse nowĕṭaanyekweashoño.

LESSON VIII.

Is it a cow?
It is a cow.
It is my cow.
She has no hay.
Let her be fed.

I see a tub.
The tub is big.
Can you use it?
O yes, I can.
I can use it.

O, see my cat!
He is on a mat.
He saw a rat.
The rat saw him.
The rat ran off.

See my new top.
How it can hum.
You may get one.
Do not beg one.
I do not beg.

LESSON IX.

See! a new cap.
A cap for you.
I had a cap.
It was new.
Now it is old.

See the big kid.
It is my pet kid.
Is it not shy?
My kid is shy.
Let us go out.

It is an elk.
The elk is sly.
The dog saw him.
He saw the dog.
The elk ran off.

See the dog run.
It saw a man.
The man did say,
  pup, pup, pup!
The dog ran off.

LESSON IX.

Muh! iske natse oshtyat{huts.
Iske oshtyat{huts nasho hishome.
Hinome saiske oshtyat{huts.
Immeĕ oshtyat{huts natsetsa.

Sĕokutch karawash washtye sitchu.
Tua imme satyashe karawash washtye sotchoowĕtyo.
Imme{a karawash washtye satse kowkutseiosho?
Satyashe karawash washtye imme kowkutseiosho.
Hina showo nutyĕko chatye.

{ua imme iske {yusha.
{yusha imme kowkutsaiyawe.
Tĕya kokutch {yusha
{yusha komētsa kotye{yu thoko.

Sĕokutch tĕya komētsa.
Tĕya kokutcha iske hutstse.
Hutstse ĕkatsa, tĕya washtye, tĕya washtye, tĕya washtye!
Tĕya komētsa kotye{yu thoko.

LESSON X.

Hinome itye ñyokutchse hishome musa.
Hishome musa itye ñyokutchtyuma hinome?
Musa imme eistyu tinyeyaño styuka washats soshtyattuts natse.
Yoko thoko hustchētsa musa.

Hinome sēokutch iske tēya.
Hinome ñyokutchse iske tēya washtye.
Itye hishome ñyokutchtyuma hinome?
Tēya thick tēya washtye itye ñyomētstako setyu.

Ned thick katyashe kavayo.
Itye ñyomētstyo kavayo?
Itye ñyomētstyo kavayo tyĕĕ?
Ha, kavayo itye ñyomētsko; thick itye Ned ñyomētsko.

Sēokutch koyowtsa kwako.
Satsena kwako chēshata?
Itye kwako ñyeyotyo?
Itye kwako ñyeyotyo tyĕĕ?
Kwako itye nēyoko.

LESSON X.

I can see you, cat.
Do you see me?
The cat is on my
 new fur cap.
Get off, old cat.

I see a dog.
I can see a pup.
Do you see me?
The dog and pup
 may run all day.

Ned and his nag.
Can the nag run?
Can it run far?
O yes, the nag can
 run; so can Ned.

See the old hen.
Is she not fat?
Can the hen fly?
Can she fly far?
The hen can fly.

LESSON XI.

i see an old cat.
The old cat is by
her pet kit.
The cat and kit
are on a rug.

A sly old fox, and
a fat old hen.
The fox did try to
get the hen.
Did the hen fly?

dog	boy	get
log	joy	let
hog	toy	set
fog	coy	bet

Do you see the boy and his dog?
Is it a dog, or is it a fox?
Is it a fox? O no, it is a dog.
The dog can run; so can the boy.
Now, Tom, let us see you run.

LESSON XI.

Hinome seokutch iske koyowtsa musa. Koyowtsa musa imme aihowĕko kawashtye sotchoowĕtyo musa washtye. Musa shĕ musa washtye immetsapa eistchu eistchustche tyĕka stchu ka,

Iske kowetonyeme kaiechoñyme hustchētsa mastya, shĕ iske kishata koyowtsa kwako.
Mashtya imme ĕĕko nityakonishe kwako.
Ñyeyotyo kwako?

tēya	mutyetsa	tseeina
sitch	sewēstchea	ityĕĕtsa
kochĕno	owēsheiañye	epech
heashe	kowkwetsĕta	kutyeeh

Itye hishome ñyokutchtyo mutyetsa thick katyashe tēya? Immeta tua iske tēya, komĕ immeta tua iske mastya? Immeta tua iske mastya? Sah, tua imme iske tēya. Tēya itye ñyomētsko; thick imme˙ itye mutyetsa ñyomētsko. Keitsho, Tom, shoukchina hinometitch shomētsanshe.

LESSON XII.

stchomo	the	etsetch
sēokutch	itye	him
katsa	tseaṭa	mutyetsa
ñyekutchṭoko	hishome	owēstcheaanye

Itye hishome ñyokutchṭyo stchomo? Eiṭya stchomo nyekutchṭokoñyesho? O ha! Hinome sēokutch stchomo. Stchomo eistchuka ñyekutchṭokoñyesho. Itye stchomo ñyeyoṭyo? Thick itye stchomo natsaṭyo? Stchomo itye ñyeyoko thick natsako. Ha! taah stchomo itye.

hinome	itye	sēokutch
ṭaah	koyastchokotse	ha
ah	Ned	ṭyĕĕ
eie	Tom	hishome

Ned itye hishome ñyoyastchokotstcho? Itye hishome ñyoyastchokotstcho ṭyĕĕ? Ha, hinome itye ñyoyastchokotse. Hinome itye ñyoyastchotse taah ṭyĕĕ. Itye hishome ñyoyastchokotstcho Tom? Itye hishome ñyoyastchokotsṭyuma ṭoma hinome ṭyēka? Ha; sēokutch hinome. Hinome itye ñyoyastchokotse ṭoma ṭyĕĕ hishome ṭyēka, Ned. Hinome itye ñyoyastchokotse hĕmako ṭyĕĕ kwa hishome itye. Ha! ṭaah hishome itye. Showoh keitsho shoyastchokotsaño.

LESSON XII.

bee	the	do
see	can	him
hum	fly	boy
bud	you	joy

Do you see the bee? Is it on the bud?
O yes! I see the bee. It is on the bud.
Can the bee fly? Can it hum too?
The bee can fly and hum. Ah! so it can.

me	can	see
so	hop	yes
ah	Ned	far
oh	Tom	you

Ned, can you hop? Can you hop far?
Yes, I can hop. I can hop so far.
Can you hop, Tom? Can you hop to me?
Yes; see me. I can hop to you, Ned.
I can hop as far as you can.
Ah! so you can. Now let us hop.

LESSON XIII.

Ann	ten	old
are	six	you
am	big	how
as	but	why

Ann, how old are you? I am six.
Are you but six? Why, I am ten.
But you are not as big as I am.

Ned	too	but
Hal	was	bad
pet	box	odd
pig	boy	who

Ned has a pet pig. Do you see it?
Is it not an odd pet? Can it run?
Hal has a pet hen. His hen can run.
Can she fly? Can she fly or run far?
Ned, who has the pig, is a bad boy.
Hal is a big boy, but not a bad boy.

Simple and familiar words, not found in the reading lesson, are occasionally introduced into the spelling list.

LESSON XIII.

Ann	kuts	koyowtsa
immetsapa	schis	hishome
imme	sitchu	kwae
ʃaah	sko	sekoma

Ann, hatso kusheitye shaah hishome? Hinome imme schis kusheitye. Immeʃa hishome nowe schis kusheitye? Sekoma, hinome imme kuts kusheitye. Sko hishome satse hĕmakokuʃaow hĕmakosuttyeshe hinome.

———◆▸◆◂◆———

Ned	mame	sko
Hal	mēsho	satse tawa
koowĕtyosewasho	kasha	satse tyuetsaow
kochēno	mutyetsa	howe

Ned katyashe iske koowĕtyosewasho kochēno. Itye hishome ñyokutchtyo kochēno? Immeʃa ʃua kochēno iske kwēme natse koowĕtyosewasho? Itye kochēno ñyomētstyo? Hal katyashe iske koowĕtyosewasho kwako. Katyashe kwako itye komētsa. Itye kwako ñyeyotyo? Itye kwako ñyeyotyo shĕ ñyomētstyo tyĕĕ? Ñed, howe keikoiya kochēno imme iske satse tawa eachatsaow. Hal imme iske kocha each, sko satse sah tawatsaow each.

LESSON XIV.

kaash	ka	ṭaah
kukañye	the	iske
koeach	epech	mēsho
koweia	and	Ann

Ann tseañyekwea katyashe tēya howṭyu kukañye kamasṭye keianaṭye. Tēya etsetch kwae sĕchañyeshe. Tēya howṭyu etsetch kamasṭye kaashtyu. Hishome satse chokutch tēya? Tēya howṭyu satse iska kamasṭye nowe howṭyu kamasṭye kukañye etsetch.

---

suña	ṭyĕĕ	keiṭhoa
seeina	koweṭoñyeme	koweiskuṭyetsṭa
kaikoiya	komēts	sēokutch
tēya	hishome	stchomo

Itye tēya nityaṭyo suña? Pokutch, sēokutch, kwae kaiechonye koweṭoñyeme immetsa tēya. Ah, wa keitsho tēya kaikoiya suña. Hishome chokutch komētsṭa suña? Ñyomētsṭyo suña ṭyĕĕ? Tēya satse seoṭyemēṭyo omētse ṭyĕĕ. Tēya sitya suña.

LESSON XIV.

lap	its	as
red	the	one
did	put	was
bid	and	Ann

Ann bid her dog put up its red paw.
The dog did as it was bid. It put its paw in her lap. Did you not see it?
It put up no paw but the red one.

---

rat	far	fee
get	sly	lee
has	run	see
dog	you	bee

Can the dog get the rat? See, see, how sly he is.
Ah, now he has the rat. Did you see the rat run? Did it run far?
The dog did not let it run far. The dog did get the rat.

LESSON XV.

is	fat	let	lay
us	sty	fed	ray
my	not	bit	say
the	pig	now	pay

I see a dog. The dog bit my pig.
Is my pig in the sty? Let us see.
The dog can not see my pig now.
Let the fat old pig be fed.

boy	lid	off	ill
put	sat	out	pill
box	cat	ran	kill
hen	the	eye	mill

A boy put a cat and a hen in a box.
The boy sat on the lid of the box.
The cat bit the hen; and the hen put
  out the eye of the cat.
The boy got off the lid of the box. The
  cat got out and ran off.

LESSON XV.

imme	kishaḷa	ḷo pech	eipecha
hinometitch	seiyastchema	pityesha	keispechaṭye
sashe	satse	kako	ĕkatsa
the	kochĕno	weie	petsoa

Hinome sēokutch iske tēya. Tēya kako satyashe kochĕno. Immeḷa satyashe kochĕno eikeia seiyastchema? Hanye showoh hinometitch ñyokchana. Tēya satse itye ñyokutchshoño satyashe kochĕno weie. Pityesha kishaḷa hustchĕtsa kochĕno imme paowyaḷa.

---

mutyetsa	aastche	ṭyĕĕ	sewasa
epech	kokwea	chaṭye	wawa koḷots
kasha	musa	komĕts	kaowḷa
kwako	the	howanaañye	aḷyewañye

Iske mutyetsa anutseponeie iske musa thick iske kwako kasha ṭyēkañuh. Mutyetsa kokwea eistchu aastche kasha ṭyēka stchu. Musa kako kwako, shĕ kwako kowanaṭyeko musa. Mutyetsa saaḷa aastche kasha. Musa thoko chaṭye shĕ komēsa ṭyĕĕ.

LESSON XVI.

sewasa	ṭaah	she	kaeitse
mame	the	epech	koshṭo
tseeina	komēts	ashañye	kaiastche
kwako	oshatcha	mēsho	stchatchu

Kwako mēsho mame sewasa satse itye ñyeput-ṭyekoño; sko kwako satse mame sewasako satse ñyosṭokoño. Kwako eistyu kaah ashañye sewastchañye ṭyēka stchu. Kwako eistyu kaah ashañye sewastchañye ṭyēka stchu, kaaspeĕh.

---

kaash	sṭoēts	kaeitse	seio
koowētyo	she	wĕpĕñye	kocha
tēya	(karawash washṭye)	kopyowkwea	ĕka
Ann	kashe	iske	koṭots

Ann ka iske koowētyo tēya-kaash. Ann sēohĕĕtsanye tēya-kaash eiṭyu eitsimme eistchusche ṭyēka ṭyu Ann kashe. Ann sityesha tēya seio hĕme zē kapeweshe. Katyashe tēya satse kotchow kwa iske karawash washṭye kotchanshe; satse kochaño kwa iske karawash washṭye iske seie sēanshe hustchētsa. Eisutchṭya iske sēpĕ imme kukañye.

LESSON XVI.

ill	as	she	lie
too	the	put	die
get	run	hay	pie
hen	sun	was	hie

The hen was too ill to get up; but she was not so ill as to die.

The hen was put on the hay. She was put on the hay, in the sun.

lap	tip	lie	all
pet	she	ear	tall
dog	kid	eat	call
Ann	her	one	ball

Ann had a pet lap-dog. She let it lie on her bed.

She fed it of all she had to eat.

Her dog was not as big as a kid; not as big as a kid one day old.

The tip of one ear was red.

LESSON XVII.

let	us	our	fay
hot	fun	out	hay
dog	can	new	nay
hog	put	with	day

It is a hot day. Let us go out.
Let us go out with our dog.
We can go to the new-cut hay.
We can put hay on our dog for fun.

all	oh	fit	the
for	aid	we	this
his	bid	are	that
God	our	eye	then

O! my God, let me do no sin. Aid
  me to do as I am bid.
Our God can see all we do. Let all
  I do be fit for his eye.
Let me do to all as I am bid. Let
  me do as all are bid to do to me.

LESSON XVII.

ṭo pach   hinometitch sutchaṭyashetshe pame kowweicha koēshai chaṭye (ashañya sewastchañye)
tēya   itye   natse   sah
kochēno   epech   eskawa   sechuma

    Weie imme iske seie aḷumatse. Show'oh chaṭye. Showoh choṭye nutyc̆ko sutchaṭyashetshse tēya. Hinometitch itye nutyc̆ko ashañye sewastchañye weie seotsotstche. Hinometitch itye ñyopṭyiname sewastchañye satyashetshe tēya ṭoma nowawēsheiṭyēya.

———◆———

seio   eie   tawa   the
ka   komatsanye   hinometitch   ṭua
kashe   koweia   immetsapa   wĕĕ
Dios   sashetshe   howanaañye   hamasho

    O! nashtēa Dios, pame kohĕĕtsanye hinome sotsitseshe. Komatsanye hinome ekochañye kwae hinome seechanyeshe. Sanashtēashe Dios itye ñyuwakutch skwachoma seio hatso zē esechanatshe. Komatsanye hinome hatso zē etsechanshe ṭyokochanshe kutchanaṭyēa. Komatsanye hinome esetch seio hañ o hatso zē kwae hinome choyañyekweanishe. Komatsanye hinome esetch hañ o kwae seio hañ o sheañyekweanishe ekochanye hinome.

LESSON XVIII.

mas̯tya	kishaḻa	komēts	seaḻa
hustchētsa	suña	kwako	koweḻonyeme
ĕkatsa	musa	tēya	kotsitchḻa
itye	oshṭyatḻhuts	kokutch	kuskeitsḻa

Mas̯tya itye ĕkatsa: hinome imme soweḻonyeme seiechonye. Hinome sat̯ya iske koyowtsa kishaḻa kwako. Iske hutstse sēokutch hinome. Iske tēya sēokutch hinome. Hinome sēomēts shĕ soēskomush. Hinome imme mame soweḻonyeme seiechonye satse itye iske hutstse nityas̯tyomaño hinome. Iske tēya satse itye nityas̯tyomaño hinome, hinome seomētsa.

---

kotsotsḻa	ḻomēka	to	kaeitse
kwachinñyea	sipkawēḻa	etsetch	pame
satse	okweañye	eistchustche	koshḻo
and	kustchĕtsḻa	oshatcha	stchatchu

Musa itye ĕkatsa: hinome satse ñyotsosaskoño, hinome sewachinyea. Hinome itye ñyomētse. Sēokutch hinome itye nityase iske suña. Hinome itye nityase iske tsape, tsape satse ṭyĕĕ tsēono. Hinome itye sēostchetsḻa, thick hinome itye neitscse kanachowēma. Hinome itye neitscse eitinyeyañutyu iske eistchustche ṭyēka, ko sewastchañye ṭyēka ṭyu.

LESSON XVIII.

fox	fat	ran	fly
old	rat	hen	sly
say	cat	dog	try
may	hat	saw	cry

The fox may say: I am sly.
I had an old fat hen. A man saw me.
A dog saw me. I ran and hid.
I am so sly, a man can not get me.
A dog can not get me, if I run.

sip	few	to	lie
lap	hew	do	tie
not	pew	rug	die
and	mew	sun	hie

The cat may say: I do not sip, I lap.
I can run. See, I can get a rat.
I can get a fly, if it is not too far off.
I can mew, and I can lie in the sun.
I can lie on a rug, or on the hay.

LESSON XIX.

far	lay	ten	use
jar	say	hen	man
car	may	pen	egg
bar	play	wen	eggs

The hen may say: I can run. I can
  fly, but not far up in the air.
I can lay eggs, and am of use to man.
The fox and the rat may get me; but
  if I see the fox or rat, I run off.

see	joy	tea	rose
bee	toy	kill	dose
flee	coy	dew	hose
glee	boy	new	nose

The bee may say: I fly in the air. I
  sip, but I do not get in the tea-cup.
I sip the dew on the rose, and fly off.
Boy, do not try to kill me; for I am
  of use to man.

LAGUNA INDIAN TRANSLATION OF MC GUFFEY'S NEW FIRST ECLECTIC READER.

LESSON XIX.

tyĕĕ	eipech	kuts	tawa
spuna	ĕkatsa	kwako	hutstse
kareta	itye	otyatyetañye	nawĕka
tseama	koŏshai	sineichañye	hinome

Kwako itye ĕkatsa: hinome itye ñyomĕtse. Hinome itye ñyeyose, sko satse mame tinyeae eiseshtai. Hinome itye nawĕka ñyewayaskoma, shĕ hinome immet a ciyaawe hutstse tyĕka. Mastya thick suña itye nityaskoma hinome; sko hinome sĕokutch mastya suña, hinome komĕtse tyĕĕ.

---

sĕokutch	sewĕstchea	tea	akutchtse
stchomo	owĕshaiyañye	kaowta	tsĕpakwea
kotyettye	kaowkowĕtseta	tskaah	astyeponeime
sewĕstchea	mutyetsa	natse	wĕshonye

Stchomo itye ĕkatsa: hinome ñyeyose tinyeae eiseshtai. Hinome seotots'a, sko satse hinome styuitsiptyo oweistane tea tyēya nĕskasinishe. Hinome seotsotsta tskaah akutchtse tyēka, shĕ yoko sĕo tyĕĕ. Mutyetsa, satse ĕĕkoño ñyomutyetsaskomañyesho hinome; stchĕ hinome imme tawats'a hutstse tyĕka.

LESSON XX.

Ann	mēsh kope	sēokutch	hishome
Tom	mas̹tya	sitchu	eskawa
Tray	suña	waksh	skotsip
ĕkatskwea	tēya	him	popyowtsa

|ua imme hustchētsa Tray. Tray imme iske sitehu tēya. Itye hishome sēokutch sutchat̹yashetshe hustchētsa Tray, sitchanishe tēya? Tom thick Ann sityeshe|año tēya. Tēya ñyomētsko hamatsa Tom Ann popyowtsaño tēya. Keitsho, Tray, hañye showkacha hinome kwa hañye hishome itye ñyomētsho.

Sly	kochēno	sko	eel
hutstse	kwako	|o pech	ko|awatch|a
kayawa|eie	kwae	and	ka|aka
keiyawĕĕ	weie	sekoma	kamat̹yet̹yañyekwea

Sly itye enetchako kwae seechañyeshe. Sly imme iske tēya sewasho koowĕt̹yo. Sly itya kaatch|yea ñyomētsko iske kochēno ko thick iske waksh. Sly kaatch|yea ñyomētsko iske mas̹tye ko thick iske weyes. Sly itye kaatch|yea ñyomētsko iske kwako ko thick iske suña. Iske mas̹tya ko thick iske kochēno satse natch|yeyakoño ñyomētskoño Sly.

LESSON XX.

Ann fed see you
Tom fox big with
Tray rat cow will
tell dog him call

It is old Tray. Tray is a big dog.
Do you see our old Tray, the big dog?
He is fed by Tom and Ann.
He will run if Ann and Tom call him.
Now, Tray, let me see how you can run.

Sly pig but eel
man hen let peel
met how and heel
mud now why feel

Sly will do as he is bid. He is a pet dog.
He will run at a pig or a cow.
He will run at a fox or an ox.
He will run at a hen or a rat.
A fox or a pig will not run at Sly.

LESSON XXI.

get	try	but	eel
did	use	you	feel
can	saw	low	heel
mud	now	may	peel

I saw an eel in the mud, and I did try to get it, but did not.
May I try now? No, it is of no use.
It is low in the mud. You can see it; but you can not get it if you try.

let	kit	do	are
she	am	the	now
but	her	not	why
has	bid	will	may

Let the cat be: she has a kit.
Do not go to her now, but sit by me.
Why may I not go to her now?
Do not ask why, but do as you are bid.
I will do as I am bid. I will not go.

LESSON XXI.

tseeina	kotsitchɩa	sko	eel
koeach	keiowo	hishome	kaowɩa
itye	kokutch	nutscaah	kaɩaka
keiawĕĕ	weie	itye	koɩawatsɩa

Hinome sēokutch iskē eel eikeiyawĕñyesho, shĕ hinome sĕka keika nityase eel, sko satse ityetsaow. Itye hishome nityaɩye weie? Sah, satse tsētyomaño. Eel imme mame nutseaah kaah eikeiyawĕñyesho. Hishome itye ñyokutchɩyo eel; sko hishome satse itye nityashoño eel paɩo hishome sĕka nityachoñyeko,

---

ɩo pech	musa washtye	etsetch	immetsapa
she	imme	the	weie
sko	kashe	satse	sekoma
ka	tseanyekwea	kowstcheaanye	ityĕĕtsɩa

Pame musa: musa imme kowwashɩye musa washɩye. Pame kanitchɩyea musa ɩyĕka weie, eiseapĕ sēpsho hinome eihowĕkose, Sekoma satse itye hinome weie ñyenitchɩyeaskoño musa ɩyĕka? Satse shepĕɩo sekoma, sko epech kwae hishome sheechanshe. Hinome ekeich kwae seechanshe. Hinome pame kanitchtēa.

LESSON XXII.

kopyowkwea ityĕĕtsa howe heyatsa nawĕka anamatye kua sekoma mame tawa nawĕka kastchochtse kua zē kowwaa kaiatanish keikapinye koēshai hama kwawaa kaiatanish

Zē heityetsa eikuatsishe tyĕka tyu?

Iske kowwaa. Iske kowwaa imme eikuatsishe tyĕka tyu.

Zē heityetsapa eikowwatsisho?

Nawĕka. Nawĕka immetsapa eikowwatsisho.

Kowwaa imme eikuatsishe tyĕka tyu.

Zē heityetsapa eikeiatyu nawĕka?

Keiatanish. Keiatanish immetsapa eikeiatyu nawĕka.

Nawĕka immtsapa eikeiatyu kowwaa.

Kowwaa imme eikuatsishe tyĕka tyu.

LESSON XXII.

eat	free	who	lest ·	egg
seat	tree	why	best	eggs
heat	trees	what	nest	bird
neat	spree	when	nests	birds

What is in the tree?
A nest. A nest is in the tree.

What are in the nest?
Eggs. Eggs are in the nest.
The nest is in the tree.

What are in the eggs?
Birds. Birds are in the eggs.
The eggs are in the nest.
The nest is in the tree.

SPELLING is of the utmost importance in securing the progress of the young learner in *reading*.

LESSON XXIII.

air	rice	rat
fair	vice	rats
hair	nice	cats
pair	mice	hats

A dog will bark and run and play.
A cow will give milk if well fed.
A hen will lay eggs on the hay.
A sly cat will get mice and rats.
A bird will sing in the tree all day.

cart	tree	egg
bark	bird	eggs
hark	sing	give
mark	milk	horse

A horse can draw the cart and man.
A bee will fly in the air and hum.
An ox or a cow will eat hay.
A fox will eat hens. He will eat mice
   and rats too. Ah, the sly old fox!

Always see that the spelling lessons are thoroughly studied.

LESSON XXIII.

seshṭai	aroz	suña
kwĕme stchumuts	sotsimme	suña
hachañye	añyĕtse	musa
ṭyuetsaa	seañu	oshṭyatṭhuts

Iske tēya itye seianowwatsṭa thick komēts thick koēshai. Iske waksh itye nasṭeieko hoēne tse nowya opewekasho. Iske kwako itye ñyuweiatsoma nawĕka eiashañe sewastchañye ṭyēka ṭyu. Iske kaiechoñye koweṭoñyeme musa itye nityako seañu ko thick suña. Iske kaiaṭanish itye natsako eikuatsishe sṭychu seṭyu.

---

kareta	kua	nawēka
seianowwatsṭa	kaiatanish	nawēka
achacha	kuyoṭa	kowooh
katyachañye	hoēne	kavayo

Iske kavayo itye howwe ñyeyotseko kareta thick hutstse. Iske stchomo itye ñyeko tinyeae seshṭaiyañyeshoĕ shŭ natsako. Iske weyes ko iske waksh itye nopĕko ashañye sewastchañye. Masṭya itye nopĕko kwako. Masṭya thick itye nopĕko seañu thick suña. Ah, koweṭoñyeme kaiechoñye masṭya.

LESSON XXIV.

Mary	heya oponeime	kavayo	suesish
Lucy	keiṭonitsṭa	keiskutse	(wa ṭeistche
Kitty	ñyoakwechskoma	pĕĕcha	tsēmoṭye)
(keikapinye	(sēotsipa sa	(satse	keiaṭye
koh)	imme putcha)	sotsimme)	kowskets

sitchu   sēoska   mokeicha
waksh   nowṭako   Zion
kamapa   sitchu   sityachane
koṭots   koweṭyu kosĕĕh   kwēme tawa

Immeṭa ṭua iske tēya, ko iske waksh, ko iske weyes? Sah; ṭua satse immetsaow iske tēya, ko satse immetsaow iske waksh, ko satse immetsaow iske weyes. ṭua imme iske mokeicha. Muh katyashe sitchu koweṭyu kosĕĕh thick sēoska. Mokeitcha itye nowṭako iske hutstse. Mokeitcha itye kamapaṭyēa iske hutstse ñyoṭotsko heikame katcha kamapa.

LESSON XXIV.

Ma-ry	cov-er	po-ny	lit-tle
Lu-cy	hov-er	bo-ny	ket-tle
Kit-ty	lov-er	co-ny	set-tle
la-dy	cov-et	ho-ly	met-tle

big	tail	li-on
cow	kill	Zi-on
paw	long	let-ter
blow	mane	bet-ter

Is it a dog, or a cow, or an ox?
No; it is not a dog, or a cow, or an ox.
It is a li-on. See his long mane and tail.
The li-on can kill a man. He can kill a man with one blow of his big paw.

Many words of two syllables are more simple than some monosyllables of three, four, and five letters.

LESSON XXV.

get   six   what   lie
got   you   when   die
bed   mix   where pie
sun   now   play   fie

Get up, Lu-cy. Do not lie in bed now.
It is day, and the sun is up. Ma-ry got
   up at six, and is out at play.
Up, up, Lu-cy, why do you lie in bed?
Get up, Lu-cy, and go out to Ma-ry.

red   new   the   came
has   Ann   this   same
box   was   that   fame
you   said then   tame

Ma-ry has a new box, a big box.
Let us go and see it. The box is red.
Ma-ry said it was for her: so, Ann, it
   can not be for you.
It has M on the cov-er; M for MA-RY.

LESSON XXV.

tseeina	schis	zē	kaaitse
wa tseeina	hishome	hama	koshṭo
eistchustche	keiasha	haṭye	seiastche
oshatcha	weie	koēshai	pame

Epaṭyu, Lucy. Satse na sekeittyo seschatsa weie. Weie imme sechomatsa, stchĕ oshahatcha imme ṭyĕčtyu thoko. Mary sēpaṭye stchis, shĕ imme chaṭye koēshaiya. ṭyuna, ṭyuna, Lucy, sekoma hishome kutyekei eiṭyu kuttyeschatsa? Epattyu, Lucy, shĕ chaṭye ēma Mary kaapsho.

---

kukañye	natse	the	chaatse
ka	Ann	ṭua	immeĕ
kasha	mēsho	wĕčh	saañyemasa
hishome	čkatsa	ṭaah	satse kowkutseioshow

Mary ka iske natse kasha, iske sitchu kasha. Hañye showo hinometitch ñyokchana kasha. Kasha imme kukañye. Mary čkatsa, kashe imme ka: ṭaah, Ann, kasha satse itye nashoño hishome. Kasha ka M eiṭyu kowṭame; M imme nasho Mary.

LESSON XXVI.

seshṭai	kite	sēokome
tēe	kowooh	natse
siṭya	eskawa	ṭyuitseyo
piṭya	hama	shumatsa

Tēe imme Tom thick kashe natse kite. Tom ĕkatsa shumatseshe Ned ṭyĕka, sēokutch sashe kite! Hamatsa kite imme eitseshṭaiyañyesho, hishome itye nityaṭyesho kite. Ned tsĕyo eskawa Tom, shŏ sityaṭye kite. Tom komĕts, shĕ kite ṭyuitseyo. Shŏ Tom sowhoh sēokome Ned.

---

ka	iske	chatṭye
sēokutch	ṭyue	oshṭyatṭhuts
mutyetsa	kokutch	nowe
Ned	natse	suesish

Itye hishome ñyokutchyo mutyetsa? ṭua imme shumatseshe Ned. Ka Ned iske ṭyowshtatṭhuts natse? Itye hishome ñyokutchṭyo oshtatṭhuts. Ned imme eikaacho kochĕno ñyokutchko katyashe kochĕno suesish. Hinome sēokutch kochĕno kopyowkwe kwĕme chupkuññye. Weie imme sho kwĕme chupkuññye. Satse itye kochĕno ñyomotyo wa eikaacho-

LESSON XXVI.

air   kite   line
here   gave   new
held   with   rose
hold   when   lit-tle

Here is Tom with his new kite.
Tom said to lit-tle Ned, See my kite!
When it is in the air, you may hold it.
Ned went with Tom, and held the kite.
Tom ran, and the kite rose. Then Tom
gave the line to Ned.

has   one   out
see   two   cap
boy   saw   on-ly
Ned   new   lit-tle

Do you see the boy? It is lit-tle Ned.
Has Ned a new cap? Can you see it?
He is at the pen to see his lit-tle pig.
I saw it fed at one. It is now on-ly two.
Can not the pig get out of its pen?

LESSON XXVII.

sun see west
may how down
gone why kill'ed
came soon set-ting

May I get my cap, Ned? We can go and see the sun set.
See, Ned, how red it is. Why is the set-ting sun so red?
Will it soon be down in the west?
Yes; the sun will soon set in the west.

A dog saw a rat.
A cat saw it too.
The dog ran for it, but the cat got it.

How did the cat get the rat?
I will tell you. The sly old cat was hid.
The rat had gone in-to a box; but it came out of it too soon.
The cat put her paw on it, and killed it.

LESSON XXVII.

oshatcha	sēokutch	yonapuh
itye	kwae	nutseaah
thoko	sekoma	kaowta
chate	hawēna	ñyusotsata

Itye hinome nittatye sowstyatthuts, Ned? Hinometitch itye nutyeakwea tochosa ñyokchintochosa oshatcha ñyusotsata. Sēokutch, Ned, kwae kukañye kaeitch kopuñye oshatcha. Sekoma imme mame kukañye kaeitch oshatcha ñyusotsata? Hawēna oshatcha ñyusoñyetatyo yonapuhñyeañu? Ha; hawēna oshatcha yonapuhñyeañu sonyeko.

Iske tēya kokutch iske suña. Iske musa kokutch suña thick. Tēya komēts nityako suña; sko musa sitya suña. Kwae itye musa sitya suña? Hinome shope hishome. Kowetoñyeme kaiechoñye hustchētsa musa kwēskoma. Suña howtyupo iske kasha tyēka; sko suña setyomoh hawēna kasha tyēka. Musa titya kamapañyea suña, shĕ kaowta suña.

LESSON XXVIII.

komunyesho tseeina   akutchtse   hustchētsa
oskeits   amoko   sēpakwea   čkatsa
sitcha   kotsitchļa   wēshoñye   kaishļai
čkatsa (satse sěkstcheshow) astyeponeime kowskets
kowtsutchtsa keiaļa   sepěļa   kotsaiawěļa

---

hustchětsa   sewasa   keiatah
immeě   pasho   hishome
amometsa   měsho   cheiowoh
(satse sěkstcheshow) sěka   suesish

ļua hustchětsa hutstse imme amometsa, thick sewasa, shě satse sěkstcheshow. ļua hutstse imme sēyotseya katyashe tēya, iske suesish tēya kukañye. Měsh meiko ļua hutstse imme keika mutyetsa, immeě hishome; sko weie imme hustchětsa, shě sewasa, shě amometsa. ļua hutstse satse howe keiatchshow pasho ñyomatseomañyesho. ļua hutse ñyotsipatseoma ñyeotseyatseomañyeshe kaņ yashe tēya suesish.

LESSON XXVIII.

well	find	rose	old
bell	kind	dose	told
sell	mind	nose	cold
tell	blind	hose	bold
fell	grind	pose	scold

old	sick	son
like	care	you
poor	once	take
blind	must	lit-tle

This old man is poor, and ill, and blind.
He is led by his dog, a lit-tle red dog.
Once he was a lit-tle boy, like you; but
   now he is old, and sick, and poor.
He has no son to take care of him.
He must be led by his lit-tle dog.

LESSON XXIX.

cart   this   seek
part   that   meek
dart   thou   cheek
tart   there cheeks

Do you see the new cart and the fork?
Is it a new cart, or is it an old one?
It is a new one, but the fork is old.
A new cart and an old fork.
Do you not like to ride on the cart?

lips   eye   doll
hair   eyes   gave
wax   Jane   small
blue   cheeks Su-san

Lit-tle Jane Day had a new doll.
She went to see Su-san Page, and Su-san
   gave her this doll.
It is a wax doll, and has blue eyes.
It has red lips and cheeks.
Jane has a small box to put it in.

LESSON XXIX.

Kareta	ṭua	sēeipaṭyekwea
shukasha	wĕĕ	tawa haño
ishṭoa	hishome	howapoñye
sēpuña	weiye	kowawapo

Itye hishome ñyokutchṭyo ṭua kareta natse thick omishṭoeye? Immeṭa ṭua iske natse kareta, komĕ immeṭa ṭua iske sowĕñye kareta? ṭua imme iske natse kareta, sko omishṭoeye imme sowĕñyetsa. Iske natse kareta thick iske omishṭoeye sowĕñyetsa. Satse hishome howṭyu ñyopcho kareta ṭyēka ṭyu?

---

sēmocha	howanaanye	wak
hachanye	howanaanye	sowoh
sēstchĕñye	Jane	suesish
kwisk	howawapo	Susan

Each Jane Day ka˙ iske natse wak. Jane thoko kokchañye Susan Page, shĕ Susan sēutṭye ṭua wak Jane. Wak imme sēstchĕñye, thick kana kwisk. Wak imme sēmocha thick kowawapo kukañye. Jane ka iske suesish kasha eiṭyu ñyetseko wak.

LESSON XXX.

skashe owañye   keitsaatse   mutyetsa
skashe   kamaskuucheiko   kaiatanish
ayowstyowañye   tseeina   sēoshētsa
seokome   skutyits   kowshutsa

Iske skashe, iske skashe owañye, iske ayowstyowañye, thick iske seokome. Itye iske skashe neitsaatsetyo? Itye iske skashe neitsaatsetyo tyĕŏ? Ha, iske skashe itye neitsaatseko settyu. Skashe itye neitsaatseko tyĕŏ kwae itye iske mutyetsa komētsanshe, ko thick suesish kaiatanish kwae itye tseatanishe tyĕŏ.

of   kotsotsta   seshtai   tona
tsēo   tea   chatye   ha
stchomo   sashe   sekoma   hishome
tskaah   nakutchtako keiatsa   weiye

Itye hishome ñyokutchtyo sowskuttye? Iske stchomo imme eikeiaka oskuttye tyĕka. Sekoma howkop stchomo oskuttye tyĕka? Immeta oskuttye natyo iske stchomo? Sah, oskuttye satse imme nakoño stchomo. Stchome howkop oskuttye tyĕka kotsotsta tea. Kotsots stchomo shĕ yoko tsēo. Tsēo chatye seshtaiyanyesho. Nakutchtako tyĕka thoko thick kotsotsta kashe tskaah.

LESSON XXX.

net	swim	boy
fish	swing	bird
pole	found	lend
line	round	rend

A fish, a net, a pole, and a line.
Can a fish swim? Can it swim far?
Yes, a fish can swim all day.
It can swim as far as a boy can run,
or a lit-tle bird can fly.

of	sip	air	yet
fly	tea	out	yes
bee	my	why	you
dew	bud	in-to	yon

Do you see my cup? A bee is in it.
Why did the bee get in the cup? Is the
cup for a bee? No, it is not for a bee.
The bee got in-to the cup to sip the tea.
Sip and be off, bee. Fly out in-to the air.
Get in-to the bud, and sip its dew.

LESSON XXXI.

air	duck	fast
fair	luck	past
take	pond	swift
make	bond	swim

Do you see the duck? Can it swim?
Can it fly too? Yes, the duck can fly
and swim. It can fly far.
It can swim in the pond, or fly in the air.
The duck can swim in the pond all day.

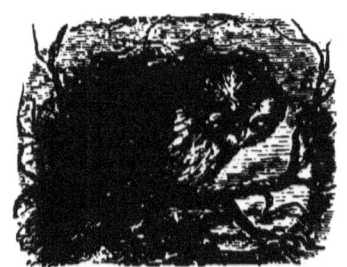

oak	owl	aft-er
saw	gun	raft-er
was	tree	sun-set
said	shot	sit-ting

An owl was sit-ting in an oak tree.
The owl can not see by day; but it can
see aft-er sun-set.
A boy saw the owl, and said to a man,
An owl is in the top of the oak.
The man got his gun and shot the owl.

LAGUNA INDIAN TRANSLATION OF
MC GUFFEY'S NEW FIRST ECLECTIC READER

LESSON XXXI.

seshṭai	wayosho	hawēna
kweme schumuts	kowyĕĕ	scaṭyu
keiowoh	koweiañyesho	seeí
koeach	keimatshe	keitsaatse

Itye hishome ñyokutchṭyo wayosho? Itye wayosho neitsaatseyoṭyo? Itye wayosho ñyeyoṭyo thick? Ha wayosho itye ñyeyoko shĕ neitsaatseko thick. Wayosho itye ñyeyoko ṭyĕĕ. Wayosho itye neitsaatseko eikoweiañyesho, ko ñyeyoko eiseshṭaiyanyesho. Wayosho itye neitsaatseko eikoweiañyesho seṭyu.

---

hapañye	kokop	hamasho
kokutch	ocheiots	pachama
mēsho	kua	keispechaṭya
ĕkatsa	kochciots	kokwea

Iske kokop imme eisṭyuka iske kuatsishe hapañye. Kokop satse itye nēkañyekweakoño sechumatse; sko kokop itye nēkañyekweako kopunye oshatcha. Iske mutyetsa kokutch kokop, shĕ kope iske hutstse, Iske kokop imme eistchuka kuatsishe stchu hapañye. Shĕ hutstse keiowooh kowcheiots shĕ kocheiots kokop.

LESSON XXXII.

tyĕñye	kokutch	kowetyumechañye
beer	china	seochawañye
haweēma	nutseae	keiotse
howeputta	koskuttye	ĕkatsa

O Tom, haweēma shĕ pokutch tyĕñye. tyĕñye tyēka? Sekoma, Ned, immeta wĕĕ iske tyĕñye? Ha, wĕĕ imme iske tyĕñye. Satse itye hishome ñyokutchtyomo? Satse na tyĕñye imme mame kowkutseiowo thick kaiechonye? tyĕñye howethok nutseae eichina nakop koskuttye.

Jane	kochacha	Sam
amomatsa	eisitch	suesish
keiowo	nutsatye	keiokei
keiatsa	naskeine	keiokei

Amometsa Jane! Kashe wak imme kaowkaiotse. Suesish Sam Page imme eikeiatsa. Jane totsetch kashe wak, shĕ Sam Page kota wak. Sam Page eichokwea wak einutsatyañu; shĕ weie wak imme keiokei. Wak kashe kunaskeitoa imme yoko kaeich. Satse itye hishome ñyokutchtyo wak kunaskeitoa eie nutsatye?

LESSON XXXII.

deer	look	to-ken
beer	brook	sto-len
come	down	bro-ken
some	drink	spo-ken

O Tom, come and look at the deer.
At the deer? Why, Ned, is that a deer?
Yes, it is a deer. Can you not see?
Does not the deer look wild and shy?
He has come down to the brook to drink.

Jane	fall	Sam
poor	left	lit-tle
took	floor	broke
room	head	bro-ken

Poor Jane! Her doll is bro-ken.
Lit-tle Sam Page was in the room.
Jane had left her doll, and he took it.
He let it fall on the floor; and now it
　is bro-ken. Its head is bro-ken off.
Do you not see it on the floor?

LESSON XXXIII.

mel-on	fol-ly	play	o-ver
fel-on	sor-ry	clay	ro-ver
lem-on	sol-id	slay	do-ver
wag-on	cop-y	stay	clo-ver

saw	tree	found
lost	took	ver-y
nest	were	sor-ry
eggs	plum	seems

Has the poor bird lost her nest?
See how sad and sor-ry she seems.
Lit-tle Sam Page saw the nest.
He found it in a plum tree, and took it.
He took it for the eggs that were in it.
Was he not a ver-y, ver-y bad boy?

LESSON XXXI.

melone	satse kosomo	koēshai	eiyoe
sotsetsetch	kotsitchḷa	hatse	ḷokanitchtēa
lemon	keio	kaowḷa	dover
karo	sityachane	hatsomasho	kopewewa

kokutch	kua	wa tseeina
keiawanishe	keiowooh	mame
kowaah	immetsapa	kotsitchḷa
nawēka	sirawĕ	kokutch

Imme keiawanishe amooh kaiatanish katyashe kowaatsishe? Pokutch kwae kotsitchḷa thick satse sewĕstchea immetsa kaiatanish. Suesish Sam Page kokutch kowaah. Sam Page tseeina kowaah eityuka kuatsishe styuka sirawĕ, thick chaowasha kowaah. Sam Page cheiowo kowaah nako nawēka zē immetsapa eityuka kowaah. Satse na immetsaow Sam Page iske mame, mame sa kweḷonyemishe each?

LESSON XXXIV.

owasṭañye	tyeeipaṭye-kwea koh	kwako hutstse	sewaṭow
mame-koso	eiṭyuoṭye	flock	koshamats
page	iska	dock	kainaṭyeṭai
sanawanye	naia	aastche	sewēstchea
gage	omoh	kutchṭyo	kotsiska

Ann	oh	imme
pĕĕsh	weie	shĕ
kutchashe	kwae	sewēstchea
sityachane	eskawa	naia

Ann hishome itye pĕĕsh kutchashe sityachane weie, shĕ hinometitch nochomosochooh chaṭye. Ann pĕĕsh kashe sityachane, koshṭyatṭhutsa, shĕ imme Ann komētsṭa katyashe tēya koowēṭyo. Ann thoko eskawa ka naia; shĕ kwae skwēstchea immetsa Ann!

LESSON XXXIV.

cage	lov-er	cock	ral-ly
sage	cov-er	flock	sal-ly
page	oth-er	dock	par-ry
rage	moth-er	lock	hap-py
gage	broth-er	rock	sap-py

Ann	oh	was
shut	now	then
your	how	hap-py
book	with	moth-er

Ann, you may shut your book now, and we will go out.

Ann shut her book, put on her hat, and then she ran for her pet dog.

Ann went with her moth-er; and oh, how hap-py she was!

LESSON XXXV.

mill	lace	light	laid
mills	face	right	paid
pills	pace	sight	maid
hills	trace	night	braid
rills	place	fight	a-fraid

lark	pur	lie
bark	like	still
hark	mat	place
mark	puss	a-fraid

My fat pup will bark like a dog.
A dog will lie on a mat or a rug.
Puss will pur, if I place her in my lap.
She will lie still in my lap and pur.
Is not puss a-fraid of the pup? No; but she is a-fraid of the old dog.

LESSON XXXV.

awañye	seokome	mashatsa	eipech
awaañye	hoawcñye	stuts	keitsoa
wawa-koḷots	sastche	ṭyeme	makutsa
skoḷotse	trace	kupsh	kowanechañye
sispeyaḷa	heitye	koweipe	seuchu

lark	katsa	kaeitse
kotseiawēḷa	koskeio	pestcheko
kachachaṭyaya	eistchustche	heitye
kweṭyumechañye	musa	seuchu

Satyashe kishaḷa tēya wasṭye itye nutseiawēḷako ḷaah iske tēya. Iske tēya itye eitinyeṭyu kaeitse iske seshchatsa ko thick iske washats itye kaeitse. Musa itye kuyoḷa, shĕ hinome ṭyushaḷaawe musa eistchu shaah satyashe. Musa makoko pestycko ncitscko eistchu shaah satyashe shĕ thick kuyoḷa. Satse sēotshosho musa tēya washṭye ṭyĕka? Sah; sko musa sēotsho hustchētsa tēya.

LESSON XXXVI.

shota-huts-tse	wawashow-chañye	kohotsa	howse kaas-tche
otyekona	kowmotsta	seoyastostotsta pittya	
wetyetsatse	kochowa	seyaawa pa-katchuittye	
tyunamats	koowētyo	katittyo otsemastcheme	
pischañye	kanaschochoe	kweichopitsta	kwēcho-kos

kaiatanish	tseeinokwea	kuyota
pokutch	kochowa	satse tsēpeio
koowētyo	seaña	kechatchoa
musa	satse tawa	kaiyotsetsa

Itye hishome ñyokutchtyo musa thick satyatyemishe koowētyo kaiatanish? Haah musa tseeino kaiatanish, musa nówtako kaiatanish. Musa itye nityako tseaña; stchĕ tseaña skowachawaya shĕ tscaña wēchintsckwea hinometitch tyēka. Sko musa satse itye sityako satyashetshe koowētyo kaiatanish. Kaiatanish kuyota, shĕ sachatchoa hinometitch kayotsetse.

LESSON XXXVI.

gan-der	heal	crip-ple	latch
pan-der	peal	dim-ple	catch
dan-der	steal	pim-ple	batch
hin-der	dear	sim-ple	patch
cin-der	clear	rip-ple	match

bird	gets	sings
look	steal	wake
dear	mice	wakes
puss	harm	morn-ing

Do you see puss and our pet bird?
If puss gets the bird, she will kill it.
Puss may catch the mice; for they steal and do us harm.
But puss must not have our dear bird.
It sings and wakes us in the morn-ing

LESSON XXXVII.

peach	fine	ly-ing
beach	nice	fly-ing
reach	large	fry-ing
teach	what	try-ing

O Ma-ry, do come and see the peach!
Is it not a nice large one?
Is the peach for me, or is it for you?
It is not for you or me. It is for Lu-cy.
Ah! what a fine peach Lu-cy will have.

ah	eye	o-pen
bird	eyes	ly-ing
were	since	mo-ment
down	clos'ed	sleep-ing

Ah! see the sly puss ly-ing down.
How still she is: her eyes are closed;
  but puss is not sleep-ing.
A mo-ment since her eyes were o-pen.
If she can, she will get our bird.
O! do not let puss get our bird.

LESSON XXXVII.

loraz	sițyumishe	kwepĕțyița
sinowts	keikapinye	tscața
tsipcheia	sitchu	keinița
skosomeshța	zē	kockchinkwea

O Mary, haweēma shĕ pokutch loraz! Satse na immeța țua iske loraz añyetse sitchu? Immeța țua loraz națye hinome, sko immeța țua loraz nacho hishome. Loraz satse imme nashoño hishome thick satse naskoño hinome. Loraz imme nako Lucy. Ah! kwae skeie añyetse loraz koĕĕ kutcha Lucy.

---

eie	howanaanye	saatawe
kaiatanish	howanaanye	kwepĕțyița
immetsapa	kē	țohatsoma
nutseae	kuuchei	sēpei

Ah! muh kowețoñyeme kaiechonye musa eițyu kaeitse. Kwae pestcheko immetsa musa: musa kana imme kucheie; sko musa satse immetsaow tsēpeiyo. țo hatsoma musa chucheie kana imme thick styuțye. Sko musa ițye, musa nițyako sațyashetshe kaiatanish. O! satse showeañyețyo musa pame pițya sațyashetshe kaiatanish.

LESSON XL.

wakune	karñyĕro washtye	kaaiko
karawash	shoeanatyu	meiko
maskokanishtĕa	kokutch	itye
karñyĕro	to na washtye	seiastchema

Immeta tua iske karñyĕro komĕ iske karawash, komŏ immeta tua iske karawash washtye? tua satse immetsaow iske karawash washtye, ko satse iske karawash. tua imme iske karñyĕro. Immeta tua iske koyowtsa karñyĕro, ko immta tua iske to na washtye karñyĕro? tua imme iske koyowtsa karñyĕro. Karñyĕro tsēwēyo kowashtye karñyĕro washtye. Kwae kotsitchta immetsa karñyĕro.

---

kowsēnits	tawa	hawcēma
sĕoska	sityesha	kanishtĕa
showooh	howanaañye	kavayo
mistchits	kutchtchashe	suesish

Hinome skotsip tua kavayo. Hinome skotsip katyashe sitchu sĕoska. Hinome skotsip katyashe suesish kanaskeittye thick katyashe kana mistchits. Haweēma, kavayo, kwēme kowsēnits. Howekanishtĕa. taah! hishome wĕ howĕchēots añye kawatyeich sĕoska tawa. Kutchtchashe kanaskeie imme tinyease kanaskeitye. Weie pityesha kavayo seiastcheme katyashe shĕ thickina pityesha ashanye kavayo tyĕka.

LESSON XXXVIII.

coat lamb car-ry
goat jamb tar-ry
creep looks a-ble
sheep young sta-ble

Is it a sheep or a goat, or is it a kid?
It is not a kid or a goat. It is a sheep.
Is it an old sheep, or is it a young one?
It is an old sheep. She has lost her
  lamb. How sad she looks.

trot well come
tail feed move
take eyes horse
dark your small

I like this horse. I like his long tail.
I like his small head and dark eyes.
Come, sir, trot a lit-tle. Move. So! you
  car-ry your tail well.
Your head is up. Now take him to the
  sta-ble, and feed him.

LESSON XXXIX.

one	stop	with
two	rest	black
cow	noon	white
plow	soon	horse

Can the man plow with one horse?
He can plow with one, but he has two.
Ah! so he has; a black and a white one.
Can he plow all day? O yes; but he will stop at noon to rest.

boy	milk	bread
cow	what	but-ter
said	gives	din-ner
your	which	dri-ving

An old man met a boy dri-ving a cow.
The old man said, My lad, what is your cow good for?
The boy said, Our cow gives milk.
From milk we make but-ter. We eat but-ter with bread for our din-ner.

LESSON XXXIX.

iske	eitopech	eskawa
tyue	koanutch	mistchits
waksh	sunatsittyu	stchumuts
otyeitsimme	hawēna	kavayo

Itye iske hutstse iske kavayo nopotsitstyo tyēa? Hutstse itye nopotsitsko iske kavayo, sko hutstse tyue katyatye kavayo. Ah! taah imme hutstse ka; iske mistchits thick iske stchumuts. Itye hutstse nopotsitstyo setyu? O ha; sko hutstse itye nowanachako sunatsittyeye shĕ nēwanachako.

mutyetsa	hoēne	pah
waksh	zē	ishatye
ĕkatsa	skowooh	sunatstyĕĕ nopse
kutchchashe	heitye	keiapotsta

Iske hutstse hustchētsa kayeieityuma iske mutyetseshe keiaposta iske waksh. Hustchētseshe hutstse ta ĕkatsa, zē heitye tawatsa imme kutchchashe waksh? Mutyetsa ĕkatsa, suchatyashetshe waksh kashteie hoēne. tua hoēne hinometitch sowowechana ishatye. Hinometitch nochape sochosa ishatye thick pah sunatstyĕĕ nopse.

LESSON XL.

natse	tawatsa	howe
añyĕtse	sityachane	sánawe
kwētse	tawatsa	kutchashe
ka	haweēma	sowooh

Hawcēma, Mary, shĕ pokutcha sashe natse sityachane. Iske natse sityachane, Lucy, chutcha hishome iske natse sityachane? O ha, shĕ sityachane imme skeie añyĕtse sityachane thick. Ha ṭaah hishome kutcha. Howe kuṭyuṭye sityachane hishome? Kutchánawe? Kwae añyeshokutch thick tawa immetsa kutchánawe.

hawe	tsē nopko	ṭyukañye
shokaka	kowēcha	shoṭa
shokaka	suesish	china
kokutch	nowya	sitch mame

Tua imme iske shokaka eskawa kaṭyaṭyemishe suesish shokaka. Shokaka immetsapa eichina. Itye hishome ñyokutchṭyo shokaka? Shokaka kokutch kwētse iske shoṭa; sko shokaka imme sitch mame, shĕ stchumuts kwae hawe. Shokaka ka sitch kowēcha thick suesish kasṭye. Shokaka satse tawatsaow opewe satse nopskoño.

LESSON XL.

new	good	who
nice	book	aunt
such	kind	your
have	come	gave

Do come, Ma-ry, and see my new book.
A new book, Lu-cy, have you a new book?
O yes, and it is such a nice one too.
Ah so you have. Who gave it to you?
Your aunt? How kind and good she is.

snow	food	loose
swan	neck	goose
swans	short	riv-er
looks	much	larg-er

This is a swan with its lit-tle swans.
They are in a riv-er. Can you see them?
The swan looks like a goose; but it is
 larg-er, and as white as snow.
It has a long neck and short legs. It
 is not good for food.

LESSON XLI.

bird   rests   gloss-y
come   ri-ses   gold-en
wing   sis-ter   set-tles
thing   pret-ty   shi-ning

See! oh see this shi-ning thing!
It rests its gold-en, gloss-y wing:
Its wing so bright with gold-en light;
Say, is it not a pret-ty sight?

Sis-ter, sis-ter, come and see!
'Tis not a bird, 'tis not a bee:
Ah! it ri-ses, up it goes;
Now it set-tles on a rose.

seal	hear	that	aw-ful
heal	haste	then	law-ful
steal	waste	these	arm-ful
takes	rings	those	let-ting
rakes	sings	there	set-ting
bakes	wings	thine	bet-ting

LESSON XLI.

kaiatanish   kowanacha   kostchemitsḷa
haweēma   ḷyuitseyo   kochinñye
koasa   sakwech   kokwea
hcityetse   anyŏtse   konupitsḷa

Pokutch! oh sēokutch ḷua imme konupitsḷa poreika̍! Poreika kowanatcha katyashe koasa kochinñye thick kostchemitsḷa: Katyashé koasa mame mashatsa imme mashatsa kochinñye; E-katsa, immeḷa ḷua satse na iske añyetse sēokutch?

Sakwech, sakwech, haweēma shĕ pokutch! ḷua satse immetsaow iske kaiatanish, ḷua satse immetsaow iske stchomo: Ah! poreika tseyo, poreika tinyeae tseyo; Weie poreika eitinyeaḷyu kokwea iske akutchtse ḷyĕka kokwea.

---

tsaaah   sekah   wĕĕ   tsē tsēocho
sēotseipo   stchastchu shĕ   sḷutshe
kochowa   ḷotsetch   ḷua   saakashe
keiowoh   katsa   wĕĕ   eitsitch
eiyaskañye   kuyoḷa   wĕĕ   kopo
schesḷa   koasa   kutchashe kotṭyee

LESSON XLII.

kayawaɬeie   koyaskowasitɬa
sityepe   koɬanitch
koɬanitch   kaiyotse
keimats   hatsoma

Lark imme tinye sutchtya tseaɬa kayawaɬeie oshatcha, Stchomo imme howe tseaɬa; Sēe katyashe koɬanitch imme kaacheia, Eistchu sityepe kayaskowētsɬa ĕkatsa.

Itye kaiatanish, shĕ stchomo, shĕ sēe, imme koɬoñyemusa, Hamatso hinome sotsimme soɬanitch? O hinome komatsanye nēputɬyesinishe kaiotse ɬyowa, Shĕ sashe noɬanitchsinishe kanitchɬyea.

---

keitsoa   sēkeishe   sekoma   yawashtye seshɬai
kokutch   oshɬyatɬhuts howe   sewaɬyo ⎰ kweme
                                        ⎱ stchumuts
stchomo   sityepe   zē   kweañukutsɬa eikowētsho
itye   kokutch   hama   osapats   komus
amoko   sityachane heitye   spechatse sɬoēts
sēotsipa shówēwēts haɬye   ɬakuts   tsēmoɬye

LESSON XLII.

meet   mu-sic
woods   be-gun
la-bor   morn-ing
du-ty   mo-ments

The lark is up to meet the sun,
  The bee is on the wing;
The ant its la-bor has be-gun,
  The woods with mu-sic ring.

Shall birds, and bees, and ants, be wise,
  While I my mo-ments waste?
O let me with the morn-ing rise,
  And to my du-ty haste.

---

fees	goods	why	sticks	air
sees	hoods	who	ricks	fair
bees	woods	what	kicks	lair
could	looks	when	picks	leak
would	books	which	nicks	peak
should	hooks	where	bricks	beak

LESSON XLIII.

girl   floor   ver-y
bird   kill'ed   hap-py
gave   a-bout   moth-er
cage   a-gain   run-ning

See the girl with her bird and cage.
One day her moth-er gave her a bird.
It was run-ning a-bout the floor; and
   a sly cat came and killed it.
The lit-tle girl felt ver-y sad. Then her
   moth-er gave her a new bird.
Now she is hap-py a-gain.

---

air	leak	licks	eat-ing
fair	peak	ricks	seat-ing
lair	beak	kicks	beat-ing
hair	weak	picks	heat-ing
pair	freak	nicks	heal-ing
stair	speak	wicks	peal-ing
chair	streak	sticks	steal-ing

LESSON XLIII.

makutsa	ñutsaṯa	mame
kaiatanish	kaówṯa	sewēstchea
sutye	howéko	naia
owashṯañye	thickina	komētsṯa

Pokutch makutsa eskawa katyashe kaiatanish thick owashṯañye. Iske scie kanaia seutye makutseshe iske kaiatanish. Kaiatanish imme komētsṯa natsaṯya; thick shĕ iske ka'ech ñye musa howethoko shĕ kaówṯa kaiatanish.

Suesish makutseshe imme mame kotsitchṯa. Shĕ kanaia seuṯye makutseshe iske natse kaiatanish.

Weie makutseshe imme thickina sewēstchea.

---

seshṯai	komus	kopĕṯotsa	kopyowkwea
kwēme-stchumuts	sṯoēts	sewaṯyo	kokwea
eikowwētsho	tsēmoṯye	kweanukutsṯa	koṯyowēsṯa
hachañye	satse-stchatshow	osapats	kokweeishe
ṯyuetsaa	freak	speṯyetse	sēotseiposo
waṯyeyame	katsa	sēokome	kaatsa
okweañye	kowweishots	yowastche	kochowaya

LESSON XLIV.

seshṭai	tsape	tyĕŭ
stchomo	sēe	sēoṭyeshu
mapañye	tĕsē	tseaṭa
weisṭañye	satse-shame	kopyowkwea

Iske tēya washṭye imme mēsh kopyowkwea iske weisṭañye ṭyēya. Tēya washṭye kokutch iske stchomo shŭ iske sēe. Stchomo satsena howkokwea iske nakutchṭokoñyesho. Stchomo tseaṭa seshṭaiyañyeshowe. Sēe satse tsēyoño. Iske sēe satse itye tsēyaṭyow, sko sēe itye ñyomētsko.

Tēya washṭye sitya kamapa ṭyēya eiṭyu sēe sitṭya. Sko tēya washṭye komēts ṭyĕŭ stchomo ṭyēka kotyeĕṭyĕ. Imme stchŭ stchomo mame sitchu, stchŭ satsena shame kweṭoñyeme tēya washṭye sēoṭyesho stchomo ṭyēka.

kokwea	sakwech	wētyitsats
shame-ĕetseakwea	ṭakaañye	seamashṭo
koṭyowētscṭa	hutstse	kokweaṭa
kusheitṭye	sotsekwea	kopeitsṭa
sañuchutsṭa	oyaṭawe	kokweeishe
koshṭyuitsho	mame-chuchananuts	sēotscipuso

LESSON XLIV.

air   fly   a-way
bee   ant   a-fraid
paw   from   fly-ing
dish   sil-ly   eat-ing

A pup was eat-ing from a dish. It saw a bee and an ant.

The bee was not on a bud. It was fly-ing in the air.

The ant did not fly. An ant can not fly, but it can run.

The pup put its paw on the ant But it ran a-way from the bee.

It was a big bee, and the sil-ly pup was a-fraid of it.

---

sit-ting	sis-ter	an-gry
fit-ting	blis-ter	hun-gry
hit-ting	mis-ter	seat-ing
sum-mer	sin-ner	beat-ing
hum-mer	din-ner	heat-ing
drum-mer	thin-ner	heal-ing

1st Rd. 4.

LESSON XLV.

din-ner	a-way
sit-ting	to-day
hun-gry	try-ing
sum-mer	mis-ter

One sum-mer day, a hun-gry fox saw a fat hen, sit-ting on a box lid.

The sly fox said, I can get a din-ner now. But not so.

A big boy saw mis-ter fox, as he was try-ing to get the hen.

The boy ran for his gun. The fox saw the boy go for the gun.

Ah! said mis-ter fox, I can not get a fat din-ner to-day.

If I am not off, the boy may get me. So, a-way ran the fox.

stay	wing	that	rives	pound
clay	bring	then	dives	wound
play	string	there	hives	ground

LESSON XLV.

oyaţawe   ţyĕŏ
kokweaţa   weie
seamashţo   sēoţañyekwea
kusheittye   hutstse

Iske seie kusheittye, iske mastya sēyamastchishe kokutch iske kishaţa kwako kokweaţa eistchu iske kaastche kasha ţyēka stchu. Mastya kaiechoñye koweţoñeme ĕkatsa, hinome itye nityase opewe weie. Sko satsena ţaah. Iske kocha mutyetsa kokutch mastya, immeĕ stchĕ mastya kotsitchţa nityakonishe kwako. Mutyetsa komēts kowcheiots kaaikoiya. Mastya kokutsh mutyetsa kowcheiots howe kaaikoiya. Ah! ĕkatsa mastya, hinome satse itye nityasinishe kishaţa nopsinishe weie.

Sah hinome sayokoţhosĕow, wĕĕ mutyetsa ñyeeinakoma hinome. ţaah, mastya komēts yoko ţyĕŏ.

---

pame-na-ēma koasa wĕē echina owĕtyeme
hatse hawecheiko shĕ-imme { koweñyeĕ- { konastchuputs   tyume
koēshai sēokome weiye stchomo-kama hatse

LESSON XLVI.

hawēna	koasa	thickina
eskaiatse	sēokome	tyuitseyo
howeputḷa	konaṭyumo	tyuitseyo
kowēñyeĕstchuputs	hatse	iska

Muh mutyetsa thick kashe natse kite. Weie kite kowēñyeĕstchuputs seshḷaiyañyeshowĕ.

Kite ñukamesēñuthoko hatse ṭyēka. O, stchĕ kite nowe iskaiatse koasoṭye!

Kite satse itye ñyeyokoño. Epech eie noweinase iske koasa imme ḷaah.

Shaow, keitsho imme tawa. Weie shaow keitsho hañye kite kowko itye ṭyu ñyeyoṭyo.

'O ha, keitsho hawēna kite ṭyuitseyaḷa! Weie sēokome imme seio seiskwesputḷa.

Hishome itye tēape shĕ pityaṭye kite. Hinome kama shĕ keieipaṭye thickina sēokome.

yaka	waksh	pañye	makutsa	sitchu
satchṭye	weie	kanñye	yaspa	kuyoḷa
keiatchṭye	otyeitsimme	mistchits	kopewewa	stchats

LESSON XLVI.

fast   wing   more
side   string   rise
some   wound   ri-ses
dives   ground   oth-er

See the boy with his new kite. Now it dives in the air.

It will come to the ground. O, it has but one wing!

It will not fly. Put a wing on the oth-er side.

There, that will do. Now let us see if it will rise.

O yes, how fast it ri-ses! Now the string is all wound off.

You may stay and hold it. I will go and get some more string.

---

corn	cow	sack	lass	long
horn	now	back	mass	song
horns	plow	black	grass	strong

LESSON XLVII.

four	cart	lies
draw	hard	works
sleep	quite	drinks
aft-er	white	wa-ter

An ox has two horns. He has four legs and four feet.

The ox can draw the plow. He can draw the cart.

He is quite strong, and works ver-y hard for man.

He has red, or white, or black hair.

He eats grass, and hay, and corn; and he drinks wa-ter.

He lies down on his side to sleep or to rest, aft-er his work is done.

---

sees	light	glow	could	east
flees	night	grow	would	feast
trees	bright	know	should	beast

LESSON XLVII.

tyana   kareta   kaeitse
hawe-tsēotseya kcio   ˈkotanitch
sēpakwea   maēma   kuskattyekwea
hamasho   stchumuts   sits

Iske weyes imme tyue satchtye. Iske weyes imme tyana kamatye thick tyana kastye.

Weyes itye otyeitsimme neikoiako. Weyes itye howeñyeotseyako kareta.

Weyes imme skeie stchats, shĕ weyes tawa kotanitch nakonishe hutstse.

Weyes imme kusĕĕh kukañye, ko stcumuts, ko mistchits. Imme weyes kopyowkwe kopewewanishe, ko sewastchañye, ko yaka; shĕ kuska sits.

Weyes kaeitse iskeiatseñu nēpatako nowanachako, hamasho seio katyashe kotanitch.

---

kokutch   mashatsa   kastchotse   itye   yonahah
kotyetye   kupsh   kētoñye   sēotsipa   pashko
kua   konuputsta   kotoñye   enctchako   atyashe

LAGUNA INDIAN TRANSLATION OF MC GUFFEY'S NEW FIRST ECLECTIC READER.

LESSON XLVIII.

yonapuh	kua	thick
kama	shĕtyĕtṭa	kweṭoñyeme
howooh	tawatch	otseṭokeie
koeach	koṭoñye	kaah

| keiowoh | pashoko | kopewewa | itye |
| etsetch | sēpei | sowaka-kochinñye | ˙enetchako |

Muh, oshatcha imme tinyeaska.

Oshatcha ṭyēya sotchowamasho, oshatcha imme koeach ñyeṭoñyekonishe kuatsishe shĕ ashañye kopewewanishe.

Oshatcha komuh hañyesaṭyu, shĕ kopo punaminñuh.

Shĕ imme komunnye oshatcha, imme sechuma kaeicha; shĕ imme oshatcha kopunñye imme kupsh kaeitcha. Shoṭoñye hishome howe oshatcha koeach? Dios koeach oshatcha. Dios thick koeach tawatch, thick seio shĕtyĕtṭa. Imme tawatch shĕtyĕtṭa ṭyēya kupshó howe eskawachañye mashatsa. Dios seiotse howoh eskawachañye hinometitch seiotse stchashetshe, shĕ pashoskwatchoma stchĕĕmishe nēskonishe. Enetchana sochosa ñyewahemaskowatchomanishe ñyotseṭokeie sochosa Dios, shĕ otseṭokeie kashe tawa owēstcheañye.

LESSON XLVIII.

west	trees	al-so
lives	stars	ho-ly
gives	moon	o-bey
made	know	a-live

| takes | keeps | grass | could |
| makes | sleeps | brass | should |

See, the sun is up.

The sun gives us light. It makes the trees and the grass grow.

The sun ri-ses in the east, and it sets in the west.

When the sun ri-ses, it is day; when it sets, it is night.

Do you know who made the sun? God made it.

God al-so made the moon, and all the stars. They give us light by night.

God gives us all we have, and keeps us a-live.

We should love God, and o-bey his ho-ly will.

LESSON XLIX.

sick	what	Wil-ly
each	blind	a-bout
which	mates	Hen-ry
school	James	him-self

| free | kept | large | thank |
| three | slept | barge | Frank |

Well, Hen-ry, what do you read a-bout in your new book?

I read of three boys who went to school; James, Frank, and Wil-ly.

Each boy had a fine, large cake.

James ate too much of his cake. It made him sick.

Frank kept his so long, that it was not fit to eat.

But Wil-ly gave some of his to each of his school-mates.

He then ate some him-self, and gave the rest to a poor, old, blind man.

Which, do you think, made the best use of his cake?

LESSON XLIX.

sewasa	zē	Willy
howe noyo	satse sēkstcheshow	howĕko
heittye	kootsekome	Henry
school	James	noyo
ityetsa	pasho	sitchu	wuĕ
chimmeĕ	sēpaṭo	china oyomunye	Frank

Shĕ, Henry, zē shokchanñyekwea eikeia natse kutchashe sityachane? Hinome sēokchanñyekwea chimmeĕ mutyetsa keisomĕshṭanishe school; James, Frank, shĕ Willy. Noyo howe mutyetsa keishome iske tawa, sitch nopskonishe. James mame nowya kope kashe tawa nopskonishe. Shĕ imme heya sewasa James. Frank ciskocha kashe mame meiko, shĕ satsena tawatsa nopskonishe. Stchĕ Willy seio kwawanachañye kwatsekomishe cic keisomĕshṭanishe school. Shĕ Willy noyo kope ṭo kwēme, shĕ sēochañye iska mina hustchētsa hutstse, amometseshe, shĕ satse sēkstcheshow. Heitye, shineichañye hishome, mame tawa etsetch kashe tawa opewe?

LESSON L.

seiastche	ĕkatsañye	sakwech
keikapinñye	nowe	koṭoñye
etsetch	katsa	kokwea
ĕkatsa	sēotsipah	Edward

Sakwech Mary, Muh pokutch Fido. Fido imme eisṭyuka kokwea, shĕ ḳanaskeiṭyu kowko iske oshṭyatṭhuts. Satse na tēya kwae iske suesish mutyetsa each eiṭyu okweañye? Ṭua imme nowe Fido. Itye hinome nowpĕṭa tēya nachape howpa hinometitch weie? O ha; popĕṭa tēya nachape howpa hinometitch! Fido, hinomtitch imme nuchape sochosatshe iske mame anyĕtse kochēno nuchape sochosatshe. Itye hishome nopĕcho iske yakuchanye howpa hinometitch? Hishome itye natcho kwēme suesish seiastche, thick. Tēya satse iske putṭa kwakutsaow. Fido satse itye katsaow immeĕ hinometitch suchatseyatshe. Sko tēya ityetsa tseyah imme itye enetchakonishe sēotsepatsha sēñyemasatshe. Edward imme ĕka mutyetsa. Eka tēya imme Fido.

LESSON L.

pie	word	sis-ter
nice	on-ly	known
does	speak	sit-ting
says	wants	Ed-ward

Sis-ter Ma-ry, do look at Fi-do. He is sit-ting up, and has a hat on.

Does he not look like a lit-tle boy in the chair? It is on-ly Fi-do.

Shall I ask him to dine with us to-day?

O yes; do ask him to dine with us!

Fi-do, we are to have a ver-y nice pig for din-ner.

Will you take a rib with us? You can have a bit of pie, al-so.

He says not a word. Fi-do can not speak as we do.

Yet he has ways by which he is a-ble to make his wants known.

Ed-ward was the name of the boy.

The name of the dog was Fi-do.

LESSON LI.

goes   a-ny   cru-el
fight   li-on   ti-ger
night   young   call'ed
sheep   strong   al-most

cave	sleep	find	beast	live
caves	sleeps	finds	beasts	lives

The Li-on lives in dark caves. It sleeps there all the day.

At night it goes out to find food. In the day it goes back to its cave.

It can kill an ox, or a sheep, or a ti-ger, or a man.

It can kill al-most a-ny thing it can find.

The Li-on will not eat a-ny thing that it finds dead.

It is not cru-el, but will fight for food, or for its young.

It is so strong, that it can kill al-most a-ny oth-er beast.

It is called the King of Beasts.

LESSON LI.

kanitchtēa	heitye	sityowañyekwea
koweiko	mokeitcha	tiger
kupsh	ȶo na washȶye	saapyowtse
karñyĕro	stchats	suttya

konaȶaiyoma sēpakwea tseeina atyash sama konaȶaiyoma ȶyēpakwea tseeinokwea atyash kaah

Mokeitcha imme kowooh konaȶaiyoma samistchits. Mokeitcha sēpaȶo konaȶaiyoma sittyomana. Noyachomana mokeitcha kanitchtēa seeipatȶyekwea nopekonishe. Imme sechuma mokeitcha thickina konaȶaiyoma sotsaȶa. Mokeitcha itye nówȶako iske weyes, ko iske karñyĕro, ko iske tigar, ko iske hutstse. Mokeitcha itye nówȶako suttya heittye zē itye ñyeeinako. Mokeitcha satse nopekoño heitye tseeinow shomotsa. Mokeitcha satse sotsnēchakoño, sko mokeitcha sĕka nówȶako nopekonishe ȶyēya, stchĕ thick nako keiatchȶyemishe ȶyēya. Mokeitcha imme skeie stchats, stchĕ itye nówȶako suttya heitye iska atyashe. Mokeitcha imme stchĕ ĕka hochinye atyashe ȶyēka.

LESSON LII.

keikeiame	sēkeipe	hamasho	stchinatsapa
pitǀa	ǀyĕimmetsa	sakwech	kotsitchǀa
kokwea	koso	kowǀoe	tsēamshǀo
kwēchokos	sitya	omo	heitye zē

Henry. O Mary! hinome weie sēokutch iske suña sitchu eie kwametsa; shĕ hustchētsa Nero immeĕ kotsitchǀa nityakonishe suña.

Mary. Shĕ titya tēya suña?

Henry. Sah, sakwech, Nero satse sityako, sko musa sitya sñā.

Mary. Satyashe musa?

Henry. Sah; immetsa koyowtsa musa.

LESSON LII.*

latch	li'ed	aft-er	e-ven
catch	tri'ed	sis-ter	sor-ry
hatch	taught	suf-fer	hun-gry
match	caught	broth-er	some-thing

Henry. O Ma-ry! I just saw a large rat in the shed; and old Ne-ro tried to catch it.

Mary. And did he catch it?

Henry. No, sis-ter, Ne-ro did not, but the cat did.

Mary. My cat?

Henry. No; it was the old cat.

---

* Too early attention can not be given to Emphasis. It is during the first year at school that those habits of drawling and monotony in reading are formed, which teachers find so much difficulty in correcting, when the pupil has advanced to the higher classes. This and the following lessons will be found to furnish excellent *drill exercises* in Emphasis.

Mary. O, how did she get it? Do tell me: did she run aft-er it?

Henry. No, sis-ter, that was not the way. Puss was hid on the top of a big box, in the shed. The rat stole out; and, pop, she had him.

Mary. Poor rat! It must have been ver-y hun-gry, and came, no doubt, to get some-thing to eat.

Henry. Why, Ma-ry, you are not sor-ry Puss caught the rat, are you?

Mary. No, broth-er, I can not say I am sor-ry she caught the rat; but I do not like to see e-ven a rat suf-fer pain.

ze-ro	al-so	liv-er	o-ver
he-ro	al-ter	riv-er	ro-ver
Ne-ro	al-most	giv-er	clo-ver
a-way	al-ways	ev-er	dro-ver
a-bout	sis-ter	lev-er	oth-er
a-bove	blis-ter	sev-er	moth-er
a-round	mis-ter	nev-er	broth-er

LAGUNA INDIAN TRANSLATION OF Page 62
MC GUFFEY'S NEW FIRST ECLECTIC READER.

Mary. O, kwae itye musa sitya suña? Sĕka kope hinome: shĕ ʇyomēts musa hamasho suña nityaʇyo?

Henry. Sah, sakwech, ʇua satse immetsaow. Musa kwĕskoma eiʇyu iske kasha sitchanishe, eie kwametsa. Suña nyomoko chaʇye ñyomētsko; shĕ, ʇo heikame, muse sitya suña.

Mary. Amooh suña! Keimats suña huts skeie nēamashʇoko, shĕ howetsthoko, keimats, seeipatyekwea zē heitye nopekonishe.

Henry. Sekoma, Mary, sah hishome shotsitchʇa stchĕ musa sitʇya suña, imme hishome shotsitchʇa?

Mary. Sah, skowa, hinome satse itye ĕnatsaskoño sah ʇosowēstcheyanshe shĕ imme musa sityatshe suña; sko hinome satse ñyokutchskoño ko iske suña kunaʇyume.

zero	thick	ēnañye	eiʇyu
kowskets	naname	china	ʇokanishtēa
Nero	suttya	sowoh	kopewewa
yohaʇye	ʇakañye	sityotse	keichotsea
howĕko	sakwech	okatsimme	iska
tinyeae	ʇakañye	kowshutʇyetsa	naia
shoyana	hutstse	satse-hama	omo

LESSON LIII.

koēshai	kamastye	keitsaatse	{ mame { hustchētsa
howĕko	yae	koeach	Willy
eskawa	koats	oyestyecome	Katy
zē heitye	sutchtya	suesish	Carry

Willy, Katy, shĕ Carry immetsapa howpa ka naia eie tseañyeko sutchtya.

Itye hishome ñyokutchtyo Willy? · Itye hishome ĕnatsatcho ñyopĕtyuma zē kaikoiya kastye shumekawaya?

O ha, hinome ñyokutchse Willy. Satse na cheikoiya Willy iske oyestyekome kamastyeñyêa? ḷua imme kokutch kwa iske oyestyekome.

LESSON LIII.

play	hand	sails	old-er
near	sand	made	Wil-ly
with	wood	spade	Ka-ty
what	shore	small	Car-ry

Wil-ly, Ka-ty, and Car-ry are with their mam-ma at the sea-side.

Do you see Wil-ly? Can you tell what he has in his right hand?

O yes; I do see him! Has he not a spade in his hand? It looks like one.

He has a spade in his hand; a small spade, and it is made of wood.

A spade made of wood! Pray, of what use is a spade made of wood?

It is made to play with. There is sand at the sea-side. Wil-ly can dig in the sand, with his lit-tle spade.

Ka-ty has a spade, too. Do you not see it? It lies near her on the sand.

She has laid it down to look at the ship. Can you see the ship? Do you see how fast it sails?

Soon it will be out of sight. Then Wil-ly, Ka-ty, and Car-ry will go home.

Wil-ly is old-er than Ka-ty, and Ka-ty is old-er than Car-ry.

right	found	wade	old-er
light	sound	made	bold-er
sight	hound	blade	cold-er
night	bound	spade	hold-er
bright	ground	shade	mold-er

LAGUNA INDIAN TRANSLATION OF Page 64
MC GUFFEY'S NEW FIRST ECLECTIC READER

Willy imme kaikoiya iske oyestyekome kamashtyeñyēa; iske suesish oyestyekome, shĕ ṭua imme oyestyekome koeach koats. Iske oyestyekome koeach koats! Sekoma, zō ñeiyoṭyo iske oyestyekome koeach koats? Ṭua oyestyekome imme koeach ṭoma oēshaiañye. Weie imme yae howĕko sutchṭya tseañyeko. Willy itye nowsotsko yae ṭyēka, kowyestyekome suesish ṭyēya. Katy thick kaikoiya iske oyestyekome. Satse hishome itye chokutch oyestyekome? Oyestyekome eisitch howĕko kaṭye yae ṭyēka. Katy añutsitch oyestyekome ñyokutchkonishe ṭyēya china oyomunye. Itye hishome ñyokutchṭyo china oyomunye? Itye hishome ñyokutchṭyo kwae hatsomako china oyomunye neitsaatseko? Hawēna china oymunye thoko satse na itye skokutchow. Shĕ Willy, Katy shĕ Carry sĕko katchuitṭyeaĕse. Willy imme mame hustchētsa ṭua Katy ṭyēka, shĕ ĕtyu Katy imme mame koyowtsa Carry ṭyēka.

---

stuts	tsceina	keiyastyĕṭaatsēso	mame-hustchētsa
mashatsa	katsa	koeach	satse-immekoño
thēkstche	tēya	hēske	mame-keishṭai
kupsh	koṭotsṭa	oyestyekome	eiatyatye
konuputsṭa	hatse	konasputṭye	kowētyitṭa

LESSON LIV.

tama	keiashat̯ye̯a	nowe	Jane
has̯tyeeñye	howkas̯ho	satse-hama	Cora
kokchinkwea	itye	koso	Mary
kakah	chimmeĕ	sityotse	Lucy
naskeine	mame	eiskutchañye	Nelly

Iske, t̯yue, chimmeĕ, t̯yana, tama. Tama makutsapa suesish, scio stchana hĕmatsapa; Cora, Mary, Nelly, Jane, shĕ Lucy.

Satsena imme añyet̯tyeshe masecha makutsapa? Kwae tawatsapa shĕ sewowstchea immetsapa.

LESSON LIV.

five	spell	on-ly	Jane
foot	class	nev-er	Co-ra
read	shall	read-er	Ma-ry
hear	three	al-ways	Lu-cy
head	quite	stand-ing	Nel-ly

One, two, three, four, five. Five lit-tle girls, all of the same size; Co-ra, Ma-ry, Nel-ly, Jane, and Lu-cy.

Are they not pret-ty lit-tle girls? How clean and sweet they look.

Lit-tle Co-ra is at the head of her class. See, she is stand-ing up, read-ing to her teach-er.

Shall I tell you why she is at the head?

She al-ways knows her les-son, and nev-er comes late to school.

How old do you think these girls are? They are on-ly six, but they can read quite well in the FIRST READ-ER.

Lu-cy is at the foot of her class now. Last week she was at the head.

One girl can stay at the head a week, if she does not miss.

Was not Lu-cy a good girl to stay at the head a week?

These are all good girls. Will you not try to be good like them?

If you are good, all who know you will love you. God loves good girls.

| clean | these | les-son | teach-er |
| sweet | school | pret-ty | read-ing |

Suesish Cora imme yañye kwatsekomishe. Muh, Cora imme eiskutchañye, kwakchinkwea kokchinkwea seisomesh╟anshe.

Ñyewapĕchawatchoma hishome kwae Cora itye yañye? Cora sityotse ko╟oñye kashe sityachane, shĕ satse hama chupkunñye howethoko keisomesh╟ansho. Hatso kusheit╟ye ĕĕsho hishome tēe nowaasonishe ╟ua makutsapa? Makutsapa imme nowe stchis kusheit╟ye seĕh, sko makutsa itye shame kwakchinkweana imme Seia Sityachane.

Lucy imme mame nutseatsa immetseshe weie. Lucy weie iska domēko sēatt╟yotshe imme yañyetsa. Iske makutsa itye immena╟ako eiyañye iske domēko, sko satse eitchuma iske heitye zē.

Satsena imme╟a Lucy iske tawa makutsa imme eiyañye iske domēko?

╟ua seio imme tawa makutsapa. satsena cheeina hishome heya tawa ñu╟ashonish kwa hatsomako tawatsapatche? Nowe hishome tawaku╟aow, seio haño kut╟yinyemasastche hishome mame amoñyemasa kutchaamasa hishome. Dios mame tawa etsetch nako seio tawa makutsapa.

---

seoyastcheme ╟ua lesson seiasomesh╟a kweche keisomesh╟añyesho anyetse kokchinkwea

LAGUNA INDIAN TRANSLATION OF MC GUFFEY'S NEW FIRST ECLECTIC READER.

LESSON LV.

muh	sēotse	kaṭyekweasu	keisomeshṭa
amome	kowweiañye	itye	kaiyowo
shomo	wėiye	kakah	nashtēa
eskawa	hama	Frank	sityotse
kowkēne	mame-eko	Brown	zē-heitye

Muh, pokutch, satse immeṭa ṭua Frank Brown? Zē sekoma howesthoko Frank Brown ṭyēka?

Amooh each imme koshṭo. Frank imme hakĕ thoko kosomeshṭansho, shĕ iske each sakweṭoñyemishe kayawaṭeie, shĕ ṭatskwea:

LESSON LV.

look	lead	cri′ed	school
poor	pond	could	ta-ken
dead	there	heard	pa-rent
with	when	Frank	al-ways
kind	loves	Brown	mat-ter

Look, look, is not this Frank Brown? What can be the mat-ter with him?

The poor boy is dead. He was on his way to school, when a bad boy met him, and said:

"Come, Frank, go with me to the pond." "O no," said Frank, "I can not; I must go to school."

But the bad boy told him it was not time to go to school. So Frank went with him to the pond.

Do you see the bad boy? He stands by the side of the man.

Frank fell in-to the pond, and the bad boy could not help him out.

He cried, "Help, help!" A man heard him, and ran to the pond. But when he got there, poor Frank was dead.

What will his pa-rents do when he is ta-ken home dead?

Do not stop to play on your way to school. Do not play with bad boys. They will lead you in-to harm.

their	game	skate	bri-dle
theirs	games	skates	bri-dles
stand	shame	school	pa-rent
stands	shames	schools	pa-rents

LAGUNA INDIAN TRANSLATION OF MC GUFFEY'S NEW FIRST ECLECTIC READER.

Haweēma, Frank, stchĕĕeiyo hinome kowweiañyeshoĕ." "O sah," ĕka Frank, "hinome satse itye; hinome soñyese sĕka sosomeshṭañyeshoe."
Shĕ sakweṭoñyemishe each ĕṭatskwea satse na sityĕkaiechow soñyekonishe skosomeshṭanshoe. ṭaah shĕ Frank soṭyo ṭyeyo sakweṭoñyemishe each kowweiañyeshoĕ. Itye hishome ñyokutchṭyo sakweṭoñyemishe each? Imme eihowĕkose kutchañye hutstse ṭĕka. Frank ṭyochacha eikowweiañyeshoĕñu, shĕ sakweṭoñyemishe each satse itye stchuṭyoko Frank. Shĕ ṭyuskeitsa sakweṭoñyemishe each, "komatsanye ṭyanaṭa, komatsanye ṭyanaṭa!" Iske hutstse chaka kutskeitsanishe, shĕ ṭyomēts kowweiañyeshoĕ. Sko howo satsinye hutstse, mēsho amooh Frank imme stchoshṭo.
Kwae natsako kanashtēa kanaia minashoh shomo kama howĕse saeikoṭye?
Hishome pasho sĕka sonyesho shosomesṭansho. Hishome satse hama noēshaiashoño sakweṭñyemishe each ṭyēka. Shĕ sakweṭoñyemishe each sotsimme howetsoñyeko hishome ṭĕka,

kashe	koēshai	skete	oṭyekeiame
kashe	kowawēsheiṭyēa	skates	oṭyekeiame
ṭyukuṭaṭyu	sēotsho	keisomeshṭanyesho	kanashtēa
ṭyukuṭyu	sawatsho	keisomeshṭanyesho	{ kanashtēa { kanaia

LESSON LVI.

sitchu	pitya	sitchu	kavayo
ĕka	ʇokuts	katchuiʇtye	otyekeiame
tyēyoskuttye	mistchits	konuputsʇa	nashtēa
kowtseʇokeitshe	soyanaka	George	sekoma

Muh ʇua kavayo tawa añyŏtse! Eka kavayo imme Jack. Satse kavayo mame mistʇyiʇye shĕ ʇokuts.

Kavayo itye kowsinits, shĕ ñyeinitchtēako, shĕ ñyomētsko. O, kwae hawēna kavayo itye ñyomētsko!

Satse kana tyēya tyacha thick chunuputsʇa? Satse imme sitch tyēyoskuttye?

LESSON LVI.

long	catch	large	po-ny
name	sleek	house	bri-dle
mane	black	bright	fa-ther
lov'ed	fence	George	be-cause

See this fine po-ny! His name is Jack. Is he not black and sleek?

He can trot, and pace, and run. O, how fast he can run!

Are not his eyes large and bright? Has he not a long mane?

The name of this lit-tle boy is George. He and his fa-ther live in this house.

Do you see his fa-ther? He stands by the fence.

George is a good boy. When he was ten years old, his fa-ther gave him this po-ny.

George has come out to catch his po-ny. He holds out his right hand to him, and says: "Come, come, Jack!"

But will Jack let George catch him? Will he not run?

O no, he will not run; he will let George catch him. See, he looks at George and does not run.

Did you ev-er ride on a po-ny? It is fine sport.

Do you see the bri-dle George holds in his left hand?

He will put it on his po-ny. Then he can take a ride.

George is kind to Jack, and Jack loves him, be-cause he is kind. The kind and good are al-ways loved.

LAGUNA INDIAN TRANSLATION OF MC GUFFEY'S NEW FIRST ECLECTIC READER

Eka ṭua mutyetsa suesish imme George. Mutyetsa thick kanashtēa kowooh ṭua katchuitṭye.

Itye hishome ñyokutchṭyo kanashtēa? Kanashtēa imme howĕko kushṭye kutchañyeka.

George imme mame tawa mutyetsa. Imme George kutṣ kusheitye kaape, kanashtēa scuṭye ṭua kavayo patyatseoma.

Howetsthok George nityako katyashe kavayo. Imme George howkowṭa shome kavayo kamashṭye, shĕ ĕkatsa: "ṭoeēma, ṭoeēma, Jack!"

Shē itye Jack nówṭyeṭyo George ṭyēka? Satse ñyoṭyetchṭyo ñyomētsṭyo kavayo?

Sah, kavayo satse ñyoṭyetchkoño ñyomētskoño; kavayo ĕko George nityaseomanishe. Muh, kavayo sēokutch George shĕ satse kotyetṭyo komētso.

Hishome hama ṭyu chokwea kavayo ṭyēka stchu? ṭua imme mame tawa kowēshaiyañu.

Hishome itye ñyokutchtcho oṭyekeiame kamasṭye ishshuya kaikoiya George?

George seuṭyekeio ṭua oṭyekeiame katyashe kavayo. Shĕ George ṭyu kokwea katyashe kavayo ṭyēya.

George imme amoko katyashe Jack, shĕ Jack mame amoko George, stchĕ George imme mame tawatsa kavayo ṭyēka. Stchĕ howe tawa hutstse koh amoñyoko zē kashe katyashe seio thick kashe katyashe amoñyomatseoma.

LAGUNA INDIAN TRANSLATION OF MC GUFFEY'S NEW FIRST ECLECTIC READER.

LESSON LVII.

tyana	katsa	tseeina	satse-hama
kaiatanish	totsetch	hatye	sewēstchea
kowwaah	sittya	sotsetch	satyumo
kwah	keiots	koso	sekoma

Fanny. O, satyumo, eika iske mame añyĕtse kaiatanish! ĕshoño kotchowēstcheaño ñyotyatye-tyoma hinome kaiatanish.

Henry. Hatyeka, sakwech? Hinome satse itye ñyokutchskoño kaiatanish. Zē kwetse imme tua kaiatanish?

Fanny. Hinome satse skoñyemo zē kwetse imme tua kaiatanish, sko tua kaiatanish imme mame añyĕtse shĕ natyase hinome natse weistañye tyĕka tyu nokse.

LESSON LVII.

four	chirp	found	nev-er
bird	leave	where	hap-py
nest	touch	wrong	broth-er
such	break	taught	be-cause

Fanny. O, broth-er, there is such a pret-ty bird! Please get it for me.

Henry. Where, sis-ter? I do not see it. What kind of a bird is it?

Fanny. I do not know what kind of a bird it is, but it will be so pret-ty for my new cage.

Henry. O, I see it now. We have made it leave its nest. Do you not see its nest?

Fanny. O yes, I do. There are eggs in it. We will get the nest, and the eggs too.

Henry. No, sis-ter, we must not touch the bird, nor the nest, nor the eggs.

Fanny. Why, broth-er? I would so much love to have them all.

Henry. But it is wrong to rob a bird of its nest. This bird loves to fly in the air, and make its nest in the trees.

Fanny. Then, broth-er, I do not want the eggs. I did not know it would be wrong to take them.

Henry. It is wrong, sis-ter, to harm the pret-ty birds. We should nev-er think of them but to love them.

> God made the lit-tle birds to sing,
>   And flit from tree to tree;
> 'Tis He who sends them, in the spring,
>   To sing for you and me.

Henry. Shĕ, hinome sēokutch kaiatanish weie. Hinometitch satsotsinñyēya sē sēyo kowwatsa kaiatanish. Hishome satse itye chokutch kowwatsa?

Fanny. Hĕma, hinome sōokutch. Eikowwatsa ṭyu seṭh nawēka. Shĕ nowaṭyow kowwatsa thick nawēka.

Henry. Sah, sakwech, satse itye hinome nityaṭa skosaṭya kaiatanish, ko thick satse kowwatsa, ko thick satse nawēka.

Fanny. Sekoma, saṭyumo? Hinome mame skotsipa natyasinishe mame ṭua seio.

Henry. Sko mame satse tawa saow nochowaskonishe kowwatsa iske kaiatanish. Ṭua kaiatanish mame añyĕko ñyeaṭakonishe seshṭaiyañyesho, shĕ thick nowaakonishe kuwatsa ṭyu.

Fanny. Shĕ, saṭyumo, hinome satsc styotsipaṭyo nawēka. Hinome satse skoṭoñyemo satawaṭyeshe skeiaṭyako skweaṭyeow nawēka.

Henry. Imme satse tawa, sakwech, heya sotsñyechaskonishe añyĕputtye kaiatanish. Satse hama itye natsotsitchṭa skosaṭyo sotsimme kaapsho kaiatanish ṭyēka.

Dios koeach kaiatanish heya natsakonishe,
   Shĕ ñyeyoko iske kuwatsa ko isk kuwatsa;
Imme Dios howĕse kaiatanish, keitshotseyaṭa,
Heya natsako shotsinñēya ko thick sotsinñyēya.

LESSON LVIII.

kuskeio	tyukoṭotsṭa	eiyañyese	haweme
amoko	koēshai	mashatsa	añyĕtse
amoko	kokutch	karñyero	howetsthoko
sa	karñyero-washṭye	hapostche	sekoma

Iske karñyero shĕ katyashe karñyero washṭye. Kwae mame añyĕtse shokutchow!

Satse hishome amocho iske suesish karñero washṭye? Satse hishome shotsipa iske karñero washṭye sewasho?

Nowēchako iske karñero washṭye anyĕtse sewasho?

LESSON LVII.

like	skip	front	snow-y
love	play	light	pret-ty
fond	sees	sheep	com-ing
have	lamb	fleece	be-cause

A sheep and her lamb. What a pret-ty sight!

Do you not love a lit-tle lamb? Would you not like to have one for a pet?

What, a lamb for a pet? Does a lamb make a nice pet?

This lamb is on-ly a few weeks old; but it can run, and skip, and play.

The sheep, or dam, takes good care of it. See how close she lies to it. Does she not seem to love it?

She does love it. She does not like to have it out of her sight.

If she sees a dog com-ing near her lamb, she will run in front of it. Do you know why?

Some dogs kill lit-tle lambs. They will kill sheep too. But sheep can keep the dogs off: the lambs can not.

Would you not feel sad to see a dog kill this lit-tle lamb?

O, what a pret-ty, pret-ty sight,
  To see a lit-tle lamb,
With snow-y fleece, so soft and white,
  At play, be-side its dam.

see	dam	leap	be-side
sees	dams	leaps	be-sides
seem	lamb	take	be-tide
seems	lambs	takes	be-tides

Tua karñyero washtye mina sho iske tyue domēkoka; sko imme itye ñyomētsko, tyunototstaka, shĕ noēshaiko. Karñyero, kanaia, mame pashoseoma karñyero washtye. Muh mame howĕko kanaia tyēkaka. Mame amoko karñyero kowwashtye? Ha hēma mame amoko karñyero kowwashtye. Satse sēotsipattyo kowwashtye tyĕĕ ñyenitchtēakonishe. Karñyero kokchaño iske tēya howetsthoko kowwashtye tyēka, shĕ karñyero hakĕh ñyomētsko yanye kowwashtye tyēka pashoñyoko. Shotoñye hishome sekoma? Shĕ mēka tēya koowatchtēya karñyero washtye imme heya. Tua mēka tēya koowatchtēya karñyero thick. Ko thick karñyero itye noyo pashonoko tēya tyēka: sko satse itye karñyero washtye.

Satse hishome chotsitchta shokchow iske tēya kaowta tua karñyero washtye.

O, kwae anyetse, anyetse shokutchow,
  Okchañye karñero washtye suesish,
Hapostche koseñyeshe haweme, mame washats
  shĕ stchumuts
Koēshai, howĕko kanaia tyēka.

---

sēokutch   naia   sototsta   howĕko
kokutch   naiatyemishe kototsta howĕko
sēokutchow karñyero-washtye satyah zē-howetsĕyo
skokutchow karñyero-washtyitch katyah zē-howetsthoko

LESSON LIX.

waksh-washṭye seio   itye   waksh-washṭye
stchatchu   kutchṭyashe pitya   sēotsho
ṭua   showētse   sineichañye howčko
nowya·   kaikoiyaña   kopeits   howĕko
sineichane wĕĕ-haño   skotsipa   seiasomeshṭa

Hamasho lesson čkatsa iske karñyero ko iske karñyero washṭye. Tua lesson imme čkatsa iske waksh ko thick kowwashtye waksh wastye.

Muh waksh ko kowwashṭye. Chineichañye hishome ṭua waksh ko kowwashṭye immeĕh añyĕtse kwae karñyero ko karñyero washṭye?

LESSON LIX.

calf	last	could	bos-sy
fast	your	touch	a-fraid
this	hook	guess	a-bout
much	wear	strike	to-ward
think	them	would	teach-er

The last les-son was a-bout a sheep and a lamb. This les-son is a-bout a cow and her calf.

Look at them. Do you think they are as pret-ty as the sheep and lamb?

We call a calf bos-sy. How shy this bos-sy looks!

Do you think it would let you pat it with your hand?

No, it would not. It would run, if you were to try to touch it.

One day it saw a boy com-ing to-ward it. Can you guess what it did?

It ran a-way as fast as it could. The boy ran ver-y fast, too.

The cow saw the boy, and ran to-ward him. She tossed her head, as much as to say: "Do not touch my bos-sy; if you do, I will hook you."

The boy was a-fraid of the cow, and ran off.

Was he not a bad boy, to try to strike a lit-tle calf?

head	strike	look	les-son
what	strikes	looks	les-sons
lamb	hook	learn	read-er
much	hooks	learns	read-ers
touch	thinks	wears	teach-ers

LAGUNA INDIAN TRANSLATION OF MC GUFFEY'S NEW FIRST ECLECTIC READER.

Eka ʇua waksh washʇye imme bosetsa. Kwae seutchu imme ʇua waksh washʇye!

Chineichañye hishome ʇua waksh washʇye nityashonishe nowʇyekonishe samashstcheñyēya?

Sah, waksh washʇye satse nowtyekoño. Shĕ waksh washʇye imme komēts immeĕh hishome nityashoñye. Iske seie waksh washʇye kokutch iske mutyetsa howetsthoko waksh washʇye ʇyēka. Itye hishome ĕnatsacho kwetsetchanshe waksh washʇye? Imme waksh washʇye komēts ʇyĕĕ hawēna itye. Mutyetsa thick komēts mame hawēna.

Waksh imme kokutch mutyetsa, shĕ komēts mutyetsa ʇyēka. Imme waksh stchowa satchañyēya, imme ĕnatsako: "Pame pitya sowwashʇye; shĕ hishome sheʇyako sowwashʇye, hinome nityowashoma sachañyēya hishome ʇyēka." Shĕ mutyetsa seutyesho waksh, shĕ komēts ʇyĕĕ. Satse mame sakweʇoñyeme mutyetsa sĕka nityakonishe iske waksh washʇye?

---

naskeine	seopeits	skokutch	sityachane
zē	kopeits	kokutch	sityachane
karñyero·washʇye	shoēts	sowʇyumitch	kokchinkwea
nowya	showēwēts	kowʇyumitch	kwakchinkweana
sitya	sineichañye	kaikoiya	seiasomeshʇa

LESSON LX.

katsipa**t**ye sēkstche kow**t**yumitch satse-ko**t**añye-chow
tawa yanye katsa satse-hama
koeach sē**t**yanawē**t**a seu**t**yesho thickinah
keikoiya satse-ko**t**oñyemo sewēstchea seiasomesh**t**a

O, zē kotsitch**t**a, kotsitch**t**a kokutch imme **t**ua! Iske mutyetsa imme ka iske osh**t**yatthuts sakow-**t**yumechañyeshe **t**yēya kanaskaistchu kas**t**yatthuts!

Sekoma 'eiyañyese kutchanye keisomesh**t**a **t**yēka? Zē imme sotsimme kwetsetch **t**ua mutyetsa?

tua imme satse tawa mutyetsaow. Imme katsa sē**t**yanawē**t**a eikeisomesh**t**ansho **t**ua mutyetsa. **t**ua mutyetsa imme tseotsipa saño**t**anitchkonishe, shĕ satse kow**t**yumitchow kashe sityachane.

LESSON LX.

must	sight	learn	i-dle
good	front	talks	nev-er
does	laugh	shame	a-gain
wear	dunce	please	teach-er

O, what a sad, sad sight is this! A boy with a dunce-cap on his head!

Why does he stand there, in front of the school? What has he done?

He is a bad boy. He talks and laughs in school. He loves to be i-dle, and does not learn his les-son.

Does he not look bad? All the good boys shun him!

Do you think a good boy can love a bad one? Can his teach-er love him?

I think not. No one loves a bad boy. No one can love those who are bad.

This boy tries to hide his face with his hand, for it is red with shame.

Can you see his face? Do you see how he tries to hide it with his hand?

Poor boy! I hope he will be good, and nev-er have to wear a dunce-cap a-gain.

God loves those who are good. If you would please Him, you must al-ways be good and kind.

shun	does	miss	bless
have	done	miss'ed	bless'ed
hope	hide	miss-es	bless-es
front	love	toss	kiss
think	loves	toss'ed	kiss'ed
stand	lov'ed	toss-es	kiss-es

Satse immeĕh eĕtye iske satawa mutyetseshe? Seio tawa mutyetsapa satse immeĕh howpa sekweaño. Chineichane hishome ishe tawa mutyetseshe itye amoñyotyo iske sotsimme mutyetseshe? Itye seisomeshtanshe amoñyomatyoma imme tua satawa mutyetseshe? Hinome sineichane sah. Satse howe itye amoñyokoño sotsimme mutyetsēshe. Satse howe itye amoñyokoño tua sotsimme each. Tua mutyetsa sēotsipa nowēskomush kowawe kamashtyañyēa, stchĕ kowawe kukañye kopotsanshe tyēya. Itye hishome ñyokutchtcho kowawe? Hishome itye ñyokutchtcho kwae tua mutyetsa kwēskomastcheshe kowawe kamashtyeñyēya? Amooh mutyetseshe! Hinome sēokame keika imme tawa ñyowtyumitchkonishe, shĕ satsena hama itye nostchatsutskoño sakowtyumechanshetyḕya. Dios mame amoko tawatsapatshe each, Shĕ hishome Dios shotsetokeio, shĕ sityotse tawa ñyĕnitchtēasho tawa notsitchtasho.

satse-howpa   koeach   satse-etsetchow tawa-etsetch
sah   seio-koeach satse-etsetshow tawa-etsetch
sēokame   kwēskomasha satse-tseeina   tawa-koeach
eiyañye   amoko   shamatsetch   kotsots
sineichañye   amoko   shamatsetch   kotsots
tyukotatye   amoko   shamatseakwea   kotsotsta

LESSON LXI.

ĕkatsa	sēotseko	atyĕmatsetch	tomaetsetch
wĕtyetsats	wak	yokotsetch	keimats
eatsanye	wĕĕtitch	sĕka	satyumo
sotsimmetsa	sēotseko	onatyestye	konaskuts

Ellen. Muh, naia, muh musa zē sotsetch! Satse tawatsaow musa! Satse hama hinome itye musa tyēka ñyewēstcheastchomaño.

Nnia. Hishome satse hama itye ñyewēstcheastchochoma musa tyēka? Kutchtyashe anyitse musa! Keimats, hishome satse itye ĕnatsashoño tua. Zē kwetsetch musa?

LESSON LXI.

told	fault	soil'ed	spoil'ed
hate	child	pull'ed	sure-ly
word	those	should	broth-er
mean	wrong	clothes	naught-y

Ellen. See, mam-ma, see what puss has done! Bad puss! I shall nev-er like her a-gain.

Mother. Nev-er like puss a-gain? Your pret-ty puss! Sure-ly, you do not mean that. What has puss done?

Ellen. Why, mam-ma, she has spoiled my doll. See, its head is bro-ken, and its clothes are all soiled.

Mother. I am ver-y sor-ry, my dear. But how did puss get your doll?

Ellen. I went to play with broth-er Lew-is, and left doll-y on the floor. Puss saw her there, and pulled her in the dirt. O, how I hate puss!

Mother. Stop, my child, do not use that naught-y word. You should not blame puss, for the fault was all your own.

Ellen. O, mam-ma, how can you say so?

Mother Be-cause, puss did not know it was wrong to play with your doll. But you knew it was wrong to leave her on the floor.

Ellen. Then, mam-ma, I am sor-ry I struck puss. I shall nev-er do so a-gain, but will love her more than ev-er.

came	wrong	toil'ed	to-ken
name	strong	soil'ed	bro-ken
blame	throng	spoil'ed	spo-ken

Ellen. Sekoma, naia, musa sotsetcha sawak. Muh, wak kanaskai yokotyetch, shĕ kownatyestye seio atyĕma tyeiatch.

Naia. Hinome imme mame sotsitchta, samak. Shĕ kwae itye musa tseeina kutchawak?

Ellen. Hinome howĕh sutyĕya satyumo Lewis sowĕshaiaño, shĕ hinome eisinasekwea sawak. Musa eie kokutch sawak, shĕ kattyetyowe atyematseshow. Shĕ, hatso sañyewĕstchĕaskoma musa tyĕka!

Naia. Pame, samak, pame ĕchatsa hĕe sotsimme eatsanye. Satse hishome itye sotsimme ĕnatsashoño musa tyĕka, shĕ hishome noyo kochotseko.

Ellen. Shĕ, naia, sekoma taah ĕkutchtsa hishome?

Naia. Stchĕ, musa satse kotoñyemo sotsimme eñyechakonishe kowĕshaianishe kutchawak tyĕka. Shĕ hishome shotoñye sotsimme eñychashonishe eisina shekweañu kutchawak.

Ellen. Shĕ, naia, hinome imme sotsitchta hinome musa sĕopeitsanshe. Satsena hama hinome thickina immeĕ enyechaskoño, shĕ hinome weie mame amoñyose musa kwa immeĕh amosinishe.

---

saatse	sotsimmetsa	kotanitch	kowĕtyumechañye
ĕka	stchats	atyematsetch	keiots
sĕotseko	sĕhaño	sotsetsetch	ĕkatsa

LESSON LXII.

tseaṯa	koskeits	sewēstchea	kowsēnits
tsēei	koawēsheiṯyea	sewēstchea	komētsṯa
kashe	sowaka-hashoēme	maēma	sēṯyanawēṯa

Kakaanye each koaskeitsṯa sewowstchea,

"ṯyana suna chupkunñye, shĕ keisomehṯansho sētsemu!"

Muh each, immečh each ṯohawēna tsekweaṯa,

Kaiapetsṯa kachuityeĕse tinyeañu hawe ṯyĕkaĕh.

Sewowstchea, mame koawēsheiṯyēa makutsapa ko mutyetsapa,

Kotsotsitchṯa skowwēshaaianye shĕ seiotse skowwēshaaianye,

Sowaka hashoēme, kaiyeiṯyeshcyotsṯa, shĕ sityachane:

Shĕ, kwae sewowstchea immečh noyo howpa!

LESSON LXII.

flies	shout	joy-ous	trip-ping
swift	games	mer-ry	run-ning
their	skates	in-deed	laugh-ing

Hear the chil-dren gay-ly shout,
"Half past four, and school is out!"
See them, as they quick-ly go,
Trip-ping home-ward o'er the snow.

Mer-ry, play-ful girls and boys,
Think-ing of their games and toys,
Skates, and sleds, and dolls, and books:
O, how hap-py each one looks!

"Now for snow-ball," Har-ry cries,
And to hit his sis-ter tries;
But the ball, so white and round,
Miss-es her, and hits the ground.

Sis-ter Flor-ence, full of fun,
With her lit-tle hands makes one,
And at broth-er Har-ry throws;
Swift it flies, and hits his nose.

"Have I hurt you, broth-er dear?"
Asks his sis-ter, run-ning near;
"Hurt me? no, in-deed," says he,
"This is on-ly sport for me."

Thus these lit-tle chil-dren go,
Trip-ping home-ward o'er the snow;
Laugh-ing, play-ing, on their way
Ver-y hap-py, glad, and gay.

cries	gay-ly	miss-es
asks	play-ful	broth-er
sport	quick-ly	Flor-ence
makes	play-ing	think-ing
throws	chil-dren	home-ward

LAGUNA INDIAN TRANSLATION OF **Page 82**
MC GUFFEY'S NEW FIRST ECLECTIC READER

"Weie iske koḷots hawe," ĕkatsa Harry,
Shĕ heya kakwech ñyoyowtchowĕko;
Shĕ koḷots, mame stchumuts shĕ mame koḷots,
Kĕspaḷatsa kakwech, shĕ yae ḷeĕka kuyotsa.

Kakwech Florence, sēotsipa owĕshaaianye,
Shĕ suesish kamasḷyeñyēya koeach iske koḷots, .
Shĕ kwĕowchowē kaḷyumo Harry;
Sēei koḷots hawēna thoko, shĕ kuyotsa sēshoño
⌊kaḷyumo

"Hinome chownaḷyume, amooh saḷyumo?"
Sēopeḷa kakwech, komētsḷa howĕko;
"Chownaḷyume hinome? sa maēma," ĕkatsa Harry,
"ḷua imme ḷomah koēshai hinome ḷyēka."

ḷaah ḷua each suesish kanitchtēa,
Kowsēnits kamaĕse eitinyeañu imme hawe ḷyēka;
Tsēḷyanawēḷa, koawēsheiḷyēya, eihēañye kashe
Mame sewēstchea, sewowstchea, shĕ añyĕh.

---

koskeitsḷa	añyĕḷa	satse-kuyotso
spĕḷa	nowēshaiako	saḷyumo
koēshai	hawēna	Florence
etsetch	kowēshaiaḷaḷa	kotsitchḷa
kaḷḷyechowē	each	kamaĕse

LESSON LXIII.

sinaḻa	ḻotsekwea	yaeh	tyĕimme
each	iske-tawatch	nowya	hamasho
sowkēne	sewēstchca	sityachanę	nashtēa-naia
sowkēneḻyemishe	keisomeshḻa	seiaṡomeshḻa	each

Zē! seioḻa ḻua sityachane? Howohḻutyĕtyu seio sityachane tyĕka?

Heitye iske tyue tawatch sēyaḻyutshe hishome satse itye čnatsashoño sityachane. Shĕ weic hishomę seio itye ñyokutchsho Tseia Sityachane.

Shĕ itye hishome shame ñyokutchtcho sityachane? Itye hishome howĕnetchatcho seio eatsanye? čnatsatcho hishome ha?

LESSON LXIII.

buy	waste	pit-y	read-y
child	month	man-y	sec-ond
friend	please	read-er	pa-rents
friends	school	teach-er	chil-dren

What! the last les-son? Have we come to the last les-son in the book?

A few months a-go you could not spell. Now, you can read all the les-sons in the First Read-er.

But can you read them well? Can you spell all the words? Did you say yes?

Then you may have the New Sec-ond Read-er. Are you not glad to be read-y for a new book?

There are man-y chil-dren whose pa-rents are too poor to send them to school. Do you not pit-y them?

They can not have nice books, and learn to read them, as you do.

Are not your pa-rents kind to send you to school, and buy new books for you? Should you not try to please them?

You must not waste your time in school. Try al-ways to know your les-sons.

If you are good, and try to learn, your teach-er will love you, and you will please your pa-rents.

When you go home, you may ask for a NEW SEC-OND READ-ER.

Take good care of your new book, and give your old Read-er to some child who is too poor to buy one.

And now, my lit-tle friends, we must bid you all a kind Good-by!

THE END.

LAGUNA INDIAN TRANSLATION OF MC GUFFEY'S NEW FIRST ECLECTIC READER

Shĕ hishome itye nasho Natse Stchei Sityachane. Satse hishome chowēstchea tyĕimme nutashonishe natse sityachane? Mame nowyatsapa each kanashtēa kanaiatyemishe mame amometsapa satse itye keatchtyemishe hakĕh ñyeyatchawanakosatyow keisomeshtañyeshoĕh. Satse hishome chotsitchta tua amooh each? tua amooh each satse itye anyĕtse sityachane nuchashe kosatyo, ko thick satse nowatyumitch kosatyo sityachane, hishome showtyumechanshe. Satse mame tawatsaow kutchanashtēa kutchanaia imme howoh ñyekwea kutchomanishe hishome keisomeshtanshe, shĕ thick ñyēnatakonishe natse sityachane shotsinñyēya hishome tyēka? Satse hishome itye ñyeyotseyashoño keisomeshtansho? Sĕka onye sityotse ñyotoñyeshonishe kutchashe sityachanishe. Shĕ hishome tawa each kutaow, shĕ sĕka shoño nowtyumitchshonishe, shĕ kutyēsomeshtanshe ñyewēstcheatseoma hishome tyēka, shĕ hishome kutchawētyemishe ñyewowstchcatsewachoma. Shĕ hishome kutchama ĕse thoko, hishome itye ñyepĕtasho iske Natse Stchei Sityachane. Shĕ amoñyosho tawa natse sityachane kutchashe, ñyotyesho tua sawēñyetseshe Sityachane howe amometseshe each howe saitye ñyinatakonishe iske tyēka.

Shĕ weie, suesish sowkēne, sutchashe ĕnachatsa sochosatshe seio hishometitch tyēka mame tawatseshe Shuoweshats

Seio.

www.ingramcontent.com/pod-product-compliance
Lightning Source LLC
Chambersburg PA
CBHW020259170426
43202CB00008B/433